NO GUTS-NO GLORY

NO GUTS-NO GLORY

by
John O'Keefe
as told by
Roy E. Coats

Copyright 1985
by Roy E. Coats

All Rights Reserved

No part of this book may be reproduced by any means nor transmitted, nor translated into a machine language without the prior written permission of Roy E. Coats.

Any inquiries regarding this book should be directed to Sunbank Publishing Co., P.O. Box 6669, Burbank, CA 91510, (213) 849-1191.

ISBN # 0-9616190-0-7

Printed in the United States of America

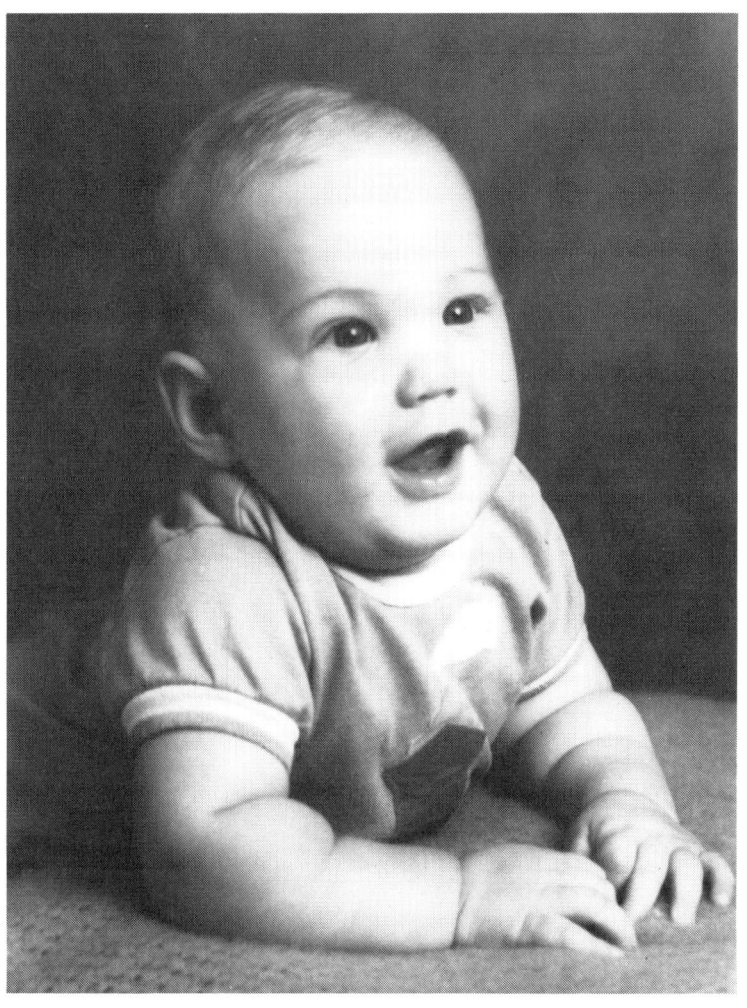

DEDICATION

I have chosen to dedicate this book to the memory of my beloved grandson, Jason Roy Coats, son of my daughter Nancy Claudia Coats. On January 6, 1980, he came into our lives bringing that special joy that a baby brings. On August 19, 1980, Jason was a victim of Sudden Infant Death. We are eternally grateful for the happiness that he brought to all of us in those few, short months.

PREFACE

"It is not the critic who counts; nor the man who points out where the doer of deeds could have done them better. The credit belongs to the man who is actually in the arena, whose face is marred with dust and sweat and blood...at the best, he knows triumph of high achievement; if he fails, at least he fails while daring greatly, so that his place shall never be with those cold and timid souls who knew neither victory nor defeat."

Theodore Roosevelt

This book is primarily about one man's boyhood dream of success and how he overcame incredible odds to make his dream a reality. It is a story that vindicates native intelligence, courage, pride in work and a sense of personal integrity.

Roy Eugene Coats began life without any of the advantages taken for granted by so many of us. Abandoned by his natural parents as a baby, he was brought up in abject poverty in Depression Era Oklahoma by a reformed alcoholic bootlegger and a formidable, true pioneer stock grandmother, who came West as a child in a covered wagon. Roy Coats literally hauled himself up from this barefoot marginal existence to where he is today — a multi-millionaire and chairman of 15 thriving corporations at the age of forty-nine.

Despite his own extremely disadvantaged background, Roy Coats believes it is the duty of those who are successful to help others, to give something back to America in exchange for their success. The result is a very American story about the willingness to dream, to dare, to struggle to make dreams come true. That is also the stuff that great civilizations are made from and nowhere is this more true than in America.

While this book details the attitudes and achievements of one particular man, it is my belief that Roy Coats is representative of a great many more unknown but highly successful men and women in America who are, in truth, the unsung heroes of society. They are the builders and movers; their entrepreneurship fuels our society with job and goods and services and opportunities.

They are not the jet-setting financiers who scuttle off to Switzerland with the company assets. The swindlers and con-men, the corrupt and power hungry, will always be with us, as will those who parasitically publicize and exploit their lives to try and convince us that all achievement and success is a sham — that success and the pursuit of success leads only to frustration, insecurity, the abandonment of ethics or the analyst's couch and other disasters. Nor are they of the dog-eat-dog school of social Darwinism or the "Think and Grow Rich" apostles. As Justice Holmes once wrote: "The world longs for some cheap and agreeable substitute for hard work and welcomes every promise. So humbug has the most friends."

What this book attempts to show is that the application of some very basic principles can lead to unqualified success and a lasting sense of pride and achievement. What makes this story particularly relevant today is that Roy Coats' success has been achieved against overwhelming odds by the application of plain old-fashioned guts, persistance, a commitment to quality and unwavering personal integrity.

While all men and women are not inclined or even suited to be company presidents, or to achieve some great artistic or scientific renown, there is just as much achievement and success to be found in any honest endeavour. What the Roy Coats' story demonstrates is that many of the qualities that go to make an eminently successful businessman and entrepreneur — are the same qualities to be found in a successful secretary, mechanic, accountant or in the running of a local corner store.

It is simply a question of scale and how far you wish to push out your own personal horizon or dream. Roy Coats has opened up his life in a way few successful people ever do, to show how such dreams can be realized, whether big or small.

As a very wise man once wrote: Never regret yesterday. Life is in you today, and you make your own tomorrows.

John M. O'Keefe
Los Angeles

NO GUTS — NO GLORY has been my personal motto for thirty years. Now some people misunderstand those words, thinking it refers to physical courage only, but this is not so. What they stand for is the determination to try — to dare if you will. It is my reminder to always try to do better in life, and to remind me that anything worth doing is worth doing to the very best of my ability. Any motto simply reflects an attitude. In my case, that attitude springs from the perseverance and success of our American forefathers. They were willing to tackle the impossible and see it through. Those ancestors of ours truly had their share of guts and we are still reaping the glory.

It seems to me that all too often today, people are willing to turn away from a difficult challenge that involves a measure of risk or determined effort. I don't like to see people give up on themselves that easily — convince themselves they cannot possibly do something without even attempting to find out. Sure, every person needs to find his or her best level of success or achievement in life. And that applies equally to a truck driver, an office worker, engineer, or the president of a large corporation. What I do strongly believe, though, is that as you learn and progress you can reach higher levels of proficiency and success than you once thought possible. It all comes down to being willing to try.

What I hope is that some people will also find strength in those words, No Guts — No Glory. That they will be stimulated to tackle things that may seem unattainable today. Our nation was built around ideals such as honesty, hard work and a pride in quality. It's my hope that readers of this book will be reminded of that and find — as I did — that such ideals are still very valid and can lead to success.

Roy E. Coats
Paso Robles, California

1
THE DESPERATE YEARS

The 1930s have been called the Desperate Years and for good reason. The decade began with the grim echoes of the 1929 stock market crash still ringing across the land and ended with the crash and terror of bombs and guns as the world reeled into World War II.

For many Americans it was a grim time. The Great Depression felled high and low alike. Men who had been stockbrokers, engineers, clerks and owners of businesses, huddled on street corners to sell polished apples for a nickel. But along with the fierce struggle for survival a social revolution was taking place as a new style of government tried to rebuild the nation. It was also a time of great individualism and excitement, of people getting mad at the way the bottom had dropped out of their lives and hungrily searching for new values, new solutions.

1935 was not only the halfway point in the decade but a pivotal year for America and much of the world. 1935 heralded an end to many old ways of life and the beginning of many new things — some good and some not so good.

In Germany, the twisted dreams of an embittered ex-corporal were taking shape as Hitler's fascist grip tightened and the order to draft men into the military went out all over Germany. It was also the year Italian troops invaded helpless Ethiopia, but in America the eyes of the nation were still turned inward to its own problems.

In Washington that year of 1935, Secretary of State Cordell Hull said that the U.S. would adopt a policy of strict neutrality. In January, raging floods caused widespread devastation and loss of life in Tennessee, Arkansas and Mississippi. March saw the Harlem riot. Dutch Schultz was gunned down by Charlie (The Bug) Workman of Murder Inc., because Dutch had wanted to kill New York special prosecutor Thomas E. Dewey. Babe Ruth finally left the Yankees and went home to Boston to manage the Braves. In New York, four alcoholics got a grip on themselves long enough to get the bright idea of forming Alcoholics Anonymous. Jim Braddock was World Heavyweight Champion, but Joe Louis was hot on his tail after a devastating win over Primo Carnera. 1935 was also the year we threw away the chance for a ten-year lead in the rocket race to come, when the government refused support to Professor Robert M. Goddard, the rocket genius.

Across the land, fires burned in hobo camps and dispirited men and women waited in long soup lines. It cost a nickel to ride the New York subway, 37 cents for a pound of fancy creamery butter and 25 cents for two pounds of coffee. Gasoline was 10 cents a gallon and prime rib beef 36 cents a pound, but few could afford either. An unknown runner named Jesse Owens was practicing for the upcoming 1936 Olympics in Berlin, and the whole country mourned the untimely death of humorist Will Rogers in an Alaskan plane crash.

That year was also the climax of the great drought that turned the once fertile states of Arkansas, Oklahoma, Kansas, Missouri and Texas into the Dust Bowl states.

In April, more of the terrible dust storms hit the area, forcing additional thousands to flee their homes and farms in a tragic mass migration that Nobel Prize winner John Steinbeck later immortalized in his book, *The Grapes of Wrath*. Awesome and frightening, the rolling walls of dust shut out sunlight, brought darkness to the land at midday. On April 14, the day of the Black Blizzard, people in Oklahoma's Dust Bowl became lost in their own backyards, cattle were blinded and ran in circles until they died of exhaustion or suffocation from the choking dust.

And, among many endings and new beginnings that year, was the birth of Roy Eugene Coats in Sulphur Springs, Oklahoma, a small settlement just a dozen miles north of Ardmore where Will Rogers, another Oklahoma cowboy, had earlier discovered Gene Autry serenading passengers at the Ardmore train station and launched his movie career as the Singing Cowboy.

Shortly after the birth of Roy Coats, his father — a drifter from New Mexico who drove a truck in a small-time bootleg booze operation — took off for parts unknown. The boy's fifteen-year-old mother then headed west to California to find work waiting on tables or picking lettuce, her infant son alongside her in the fields. But the burden of an infant was too much for her to carry alone. She returned to Oklahoma and left the child with his maternal grandmother and a reformed alcoholic uncle, who surprised all concerned when he quit both drinking and bootlegging to take care of the boy.

To be abandoned as a bastard by one's parents is hard enough even in normal times, but was doubly so in those desperate years of the Great Depression. And nowhere was the depression harder felt than in Oklahoma, where the relentless drought and wind had whipped away not only the soil but the hearts of Oklahomans as well. To survive at all was a triumph. To then go on and overcome the deprivations of such poverty and haphazard schooling to become a millionaire businessman by the time he was 30 is to throw the law of averages for a complete loop. Yet that is exactly what Roy Eugene Coats did. Today, he is many times a millionaire and Chairman of 15 thriving companies. At the relatively young age of 49, he is still expanding and conquering new business territories.

Roy Coats is a living example of what can be accomplished even in the face of seemingly crushing odds. What it takes, says Roy Coats, is simply the determination to try — to dare if you will.

"More than anything, I want to convince people that success is possible if they will only make that first decision to do something," says Roy Coats, "summon up the guts to try before convincing themselves they cannot do it."

Nothing makes Roy Coats happier than for someone to say: "Hell, if Roy Coats can do it with all that stacked against him, then I can too!"

There is an old truism that says when you're down in the gutter, there is no place to look but up. In 1949, Roy Coats wasn't exactly in the gutter, but neither was he exactly all the way up on the curb. He was fourteen years old, without money and with all the family he had ever known behind him, hitchhiking his way to California to find a father he had never known. As he watched the well-dressed businessmen and tourists hurtling by in their new cars, Roy Coats began to nurture the dream that would guide his future. He determined he would discover the rules and cultivate the experiences that make people successful. He resolved to study and learn from everyone he met. And as he stood by the side of lonely highways in Wyoming, Montana and New Mexico, in all weathers, either freezing cold or broiling hot, invariably hungry and thirsty, the ultimate dream of a poor boy began to take shape: a magnificent home set amid his own ranchland. It was a dream to wipe away the sting of a poverty-stricken childhood spent in tar paper shacks and huddled tenement buildings, overlaid with the grime and stench of nearby meat-packing plants.

Today there are many places Roy Coats can call home: his condominiums in Hawaii and Burbank, California, his house in Palm Springs. But his real pride and joy is the sprawling Rainbow Ranch in the rolling hills of San Luis Obispo County, near Paso Robles, northwest of Los Angeles.

To get there you can take either the Pacific Coast Highway north from Los Angeles, through Malibu and beyond to Ventura and Santa Barbara, or take the Freeway from Los Angeles, which becomes the Camino Real, California's historical coastal highway laid down by Spanish conquistadores to link the old missions.

It is a pleasant drive, through small towns like Oxnard and preserves of the rich and famous like Montecito and Santa Barbara, whose local tax rolls bear the name of President Reagan, alongside that of John Travolta and Clint Eastwood. You drive past geometrically furrowed fields of green vegetables destined for the nation's tables, past groves of lemon and almond trees. At Atascadaro, some 180 miles north of Los Angeles, Highway 41 intersects Camino Real at right angles. It winds its way eastward through the lush rolling ranch and farmland, which formed the backdrop for the television series "The Thorn Birds," passing near the small ranch town of Creston. A mile or so further on you pass small hand-painted signs of a rainbow, and the words, Rainbow Ranch.

The Rainbow Ranch is 1800 acres of prime rolling pastureland and carefully contoured fields of barley. Beef cattle and deer mingle peacefully on the steep, stubble-strewn hillsides and in the oak-filled bottoms and steep gullies. Past the ranch manager's house and cattle guards, a road has been carved into the side of the hill and winds its way to the top of a central ridge. Here, commanding a hawk's view of the

F90 King Air — One of two planes used by Sunbank

surrounding countryside and the Sierras beyond, sits the dream house of a poor Oklahoma boy — six thousand five hundred square feet of magnificently sited natural stone, cedar and glass.

More likely than not, the tall, well-muscled man with a full head of gray hair and full dark eyebrows, who is wrestling a bulldozer up a steep grade or herding cattle toward the feeding pens, is not the ranch hand but Roy Coats, owner of the Rainbow Ranch, Chairman of 15 different companies known as the Sunbank Family of Companies. And if you wait around you are more than likely to see him jump into the cab of a ten-wheel tractor trailer loaded with finished products from his nearby Paso Robles plant and fan through the gears with all the ease and skill of a professional highway cowboy. But if he is in a real hurry, you might see Roy Coats leaving the ranch in a cloud of dust aboard one of his jeeps on his way to the nearby airport, where he keeps his Beechcraft King Air, enroute to a board meeting at his corporate headquarters in Burbank.

Trying to pin down just what qualities Roy Coats possesses which enabled him to overcome the undeniable obstacles of his early years and become the supremely able, confident and successful business leader he is today, requires a lot of digging. For all his accomplishments, Roy Coats is almost painfully modest. Even today, when strangers ask him what he does, he is liable to say: "Oh, I work for the Sunbank Family of Companies."

When I first met Roy Coats two years ago, I asked him what he felt was the key to his success. His reply is typical:

"A lot of people might say I was in the right spot at the right time, but a lot of other people were there too — and most were in a better position than I was to start a business. But they didn't do it, and I did. That's the story right there."

I asked the same question of his many close friends and business associates and they couldn't wait to point out the many qualities they recognized in the man. A very abbreviated list of these will give the reader some idea of the respect and even awe that friends and associates feel toward Roy Coats.

Roy has enormous stamina and perseverance, said one friend. He has tremendous perception and enormous aptitude. He has combined within him the best of the dreamer and visionary with the practical hard worker.

He has good business sense, said another, and impeccable principles.

At one-to-one handling he has no peer, said a close personal friend and legal aide. Roy is extremely logical and develops a rationale for everything he does. He would have made a damned fine lawyer, he added.

Yet another observes that Roy is always a professional who can organize and also delegate authority to others.

A loyal and devoted friend, said another. He is not vindictive in any way and is completely his own man — the epitome of a man's man, he added.

Roy is a first-rate negotiator, says a colleague who has observed Roy in action during critical business negotiations over the years. He is totally honest, sets his own goals and objectives, but can walk away from a deal rather than compromise his principles.

Regardless of title, Roy believes that everyone must do his share and more to make the operation a success, says the manager of one of the companies. If there is a problem, Roy will pitch in at the loading dock or on the production line, and he expects all of his executives to be able to do the same.

Typically, Roy Coats is diffident about the qualities others see in him. "It's really all contained in that sign," he says, pointing to the small bronze plaque on the wall of his office, which bears the words: "No Guts — No Glory."

What inspires Roy Coats' friends to such praise are the very rules and principles of success that the tired and hungry fourteen-year-old boy standing by the side of the highway in 1949 resolved to learn. They were qualities forged in the shared hardship of an impoverished childhood and passed on by an iron-fisted grandmother struggling to hold on to her pride as she bleached and stitched together flour sacks to cover a bare floor. They were forged in the selfless devotion of an aging ex-alcoholic who would walk a mile to return a borrowed dime and worked from dawn till dusk, when work could be found, to keep at least the bare minimum of food on the table, even though it was invariably a little more than fatback and beans. They were the qualities to be found in the tears and laughter of friends, in the decisions that were timely and the mistakes that were costly. In other words, qualities common to all of us in the journey of life. Only some people — such as Roy Coats — take them to heart a little better than most and, by harnessing them to ambition — the real fuel of America — win through to success and achievement which sometimes goes well beyond even their own wildest dreams.

Most men, having achieved success in life, are content to go their own way. They have risen above the "common herd" either by dint of hard work and talent or on the coattails of provident forefathers. Many seem to prefer to forget their beginnings, particularly if they were humble or even average. But Roy Coats has a different attitude. Despite the setbacks of a harsh and improvident childhood, he is intensely patriotic and quietly proud of the fact that, in America, a barefoot, dirt-poor Oklahoma kid still has the opportunity to achieve high success. He also believes that, as an American, he has a duty to his country to give something back to America. In this case it is to offer his own experience in the hope that others will draw upon the perseverance and achievements of that particular struggle, in much the same way Roy Coats and countless others have drawn upon the example of our forefathers, who were also willing to tackle the impossible and see it through.

2
A LESS THAN HUMBLE BEGINNING

He belonged to that peculiarly American breed of men — the drifters. A word whose origin lies in the way cattle would drift over the open range, to be followed by cowboys or drifters. Latter-day drifters seem to be possessed by that same restlessness that led men to a life on the open range. They move from town to town, job to job — a lonely legion on the margins of society.

One such drifter was Roy Coats' natural father, Eugene Coats. Another was Eugene's older brother, Bob Coats. The difference being that the birth of Roy Coats brought a radical change to Bob Coats. Perhaps if Eugene had not abandoned his infant son, Bob Coats would have kept to his drinking and drifting ways.

Bob Coats' formal education was practically non-existent, having been brought up in Indian Territory in New Mexico in the late 1800's, where arguments and feuds were still settled with a Winchester 44. He spent his life drifting around from job to job and, like so many drifters, had developed into something of a homespun philosopher and a fiery political observer. He would argue for hours over the New Deal and how Roosevelt was "ruining the country."

At the time of Roy Coats' birth in 1935, Bob Coats was in his fifties — a small, thin, wiry man, marked by years of hard living and harder drinking — but still tough as nails. He was in fact an alcoholic. Whether it was a sense of family loyalty or some reflection of his own hard upbringing no one knows, but shortly after Roy Coats was born, Bob Coats quit working for the amateur bootleg gang and moved in with Susie Blocker and young Roy as head of the small household.

He also quit drinking and from that day until he died never touched another drop of alchohol.

From that time on, Bob Coats' sole concern seemed to be the care and upbringing of his brother's child. His example of love, devotion, thoughtfulness, dogged persistence and plain guts remains with Roy to this day as one of his most precious memories.

In fact, it is not hard to trace qualities in Roy Coats that spring directly from that close relationship between the impressionable child and his substitute father.

The Coats family all seem to have been quintessential drifters. Bob and Eugene Coats were two of twelve sons, all born in the frontier Indian territories of New Mexico.

In 1935, the two Coats brothers were involved with a small bootleg booze organization running between New Mexico and the dry state of Oklahoma. Known as the Blocker Gang, this small-time operation was run by Jim Blocker. It was Jim Blocker who introduced Eugene Coats to his fifteen-year-old sister, Sephronie Blocker.

It is often said that men shape the land, but it is equally true that in many cases the land shapes the men as well. The history of Oklahoma is a vivid reflection of that peculiar American phenomenon of restlessness so closely involved with the American Dream of better things — be it better beaver skins in the next mountain range, better grazing in the next valley or a better job in the next state. Oklahoma was the last state to be fashioned from the Louisianna Territory purchase and was then home to the resettled southeastern tribes of Cherokee, Chicasaw, Choctaw, Creek and Seminole Indians.

The central part of Oklahoma, where Roy Coats was born, is mostly hilly country with forests of pine, oak, hickory, cypress and magnolia. As you travel further west you enter the windswept prairie lands, with its violent extremes of heat and cold, drought and flood and that relentless Oklahoma wind. It is as though remnants, left over bits of geography and peoples, found themselves a meeting ground in Oklahoma.

Because Oklahoma forms a kind of transition zone between the humid, tropical climate of the South and the cooler weather of the North, turbulent weather is a natural result. The seasons overlap and fight with each other. May can bring eighty degree heat or a swirling snowstorm. Fall can arrive in October or December. Sometimes it doesn't rain for six months and then a year's worth of rain can drop in a matter of hours. Air masses collide over the state and the wind is a force to be reckoned with. Violent tornadoes and electrical storms are frequent, scattering hail or sand behind them. Russian thistles and tumbleweeds race across the land, driven by winds that reach fifty to seventy miles an hour.

Sulphur Springs, Oklahoma, where Roy Coats was born and spent his early years, lies just east of the ancient Arbuckle Mountains. The mountains are a geological peculiarity, having been worn down from their original height of thousands of feet to only six or seven hundred feet above the surrounding plains. The top of the range, as seen from Interstate 35, looks as though some tremendous upheaval has pushed a giant plug of earth toward the sky, showing multi-colored streaks and layers of exposed strata.

Further east, the land changes dramatically. Here, broken cotton stubble dots the fields and unpainted shanties blend in with the dull earth colors. Yards play host to children, dogs, chickens and pigs, cast-off furniture and the rusting hulks of abandoned cars.

Frontier attitudes still linger in Oklahoma, as do memories of the disastrous Dust Bowl days and the devastation visited not only to the land but to the people of Oklahoma. There was and is still a strange mixture of peacefulness and violence, naivety and sophistication, where even today fortunes are won and lost in cattle, oil and crops.

Sephronie Blocker, Roy Coats' mother, was at continual loggerheads with her own mother, Susie Blocker. Susie Blocker was a big-bodied formidable frontier type woman. She was straightlaced and a perfectionist when it came to keeping house — even if that house was not much more than a shack. She was also an iron-fisted disciplinarian, which she backed up with a ready hand.

When her mother tried to force Sephronie toward a marriage she didn't care for, the fifteen-year-old part-Indian girl ran away with Eugene Coats. She returned to her mother's house after the birth of her son, Roy. The father, Eugene, was long gone by then.

Susie Blocker opened her heart to the young boy. She fussed over him and showed affection that her daughter Sephronie felt she had never received. This unfortunately

Susie Blocker — Roy's grandmother

widened the rift between them. In a flash of independence, Sephronie took the baby and fled west to California. Here she waited on tables or picked lettuce, her baby beside her in the fields. But such a life was too much for a young girl. Sephronie finally admitted defeat, went back to Sulphur Springs, and turned her baby son over to her mother to raise. Sephronie then returned to California alone, searching for a better life than the one she had left behind.

It was at this point that Bob Coats suddenly moved in with Roy and his grandmother. Although Bob Coats was not an "educated man," he had acquired that most valuable of assets — common sense — and that inner thoughtfulness that frontier living frequently inspires. He was also impeccably honest when dealing with others, had a natural sense of courtesy and a lion's share of intestinal fortitude. And these attributes he nurtured in the young boy, little dreaming that one day they would become the basis for Roy Coats' extraordinary success.

For those first ten critical years of Roy Coats' life, his Uncle Bob was both his mentor and closest friend. The love and affection between the small boy and his grizzled uncle is remembered even today by those who knew the family. At night, the young child slept with his Uncle Bob and followed him about like a shadow during the day.

From all accounts, young Roy Coats was a rambunctious and precocious child, but in all those years together his Uncle Bob only struck Roy once, and that was when he had been literally driven to distraction.

"It was the only time he ever laid a hand on me," Roy remembers, "and he regretted it instantly and kept apologizing as he hugged me." The incident illustrated a tender side of Uncle Bob's outwardly tough character that Roy Coats has never forgotten.

The other major influence on the young boy at that time was, of course, his maternal grandmother, Susie Blocker. As a little girl she had come west to Oklahoma in a covered wagon from somewhere in the deep South. Her life had been rugged in the extreme and consequently she was not a very forgiving type of person.

"If you goofed a little, you had to answer up right now," Roy recalls. "She was the one who cracked the whip, but I had a great deal of respect for her — especially as I got older

— and for the qualities she helped develop in me. We were extremely poor and had very little in the way of possessions, but everything we had was fresh and clean. And it damn well better stay that way or you'd have to answer to her.

"Over the span of my life I've always wanted things neat, clean and orderly," adds Roy, "and I'll always be grateful to her for giving me that."

Although Roy Coats never went beyond the tenth grade in school, what learning he did get obviously fell on extremely fertile ground. Actually, it is remarkable that he managed to get as far as the tenth grade given the circumstances surrounding his early years. His first experience with school took place in a one-room schoolhouse near Sulphur Springs, with about a dozen other children of assorted ages. It was here that Roy learned to take care of himself against bigger and older children.

Typically, the first time he came home with a bloody nose from a schoolyard brawl, his main concern was what his grandmother would do when she saw his bloody shirt. Roy snuck into the house and hid the shirt in a closet, but his grandmother found it and expressed her displeasure on Roy's hide with a hard and calloused hand.

"I was more afraid of what my grandmother would do if I came home with my clothes torn up and dirty than I was of any schoolyard bullies," Roy recalls with a grin.

Yet her stern ways and harsh discipline were in fact an expression of her deep love and concern for the boy. Her grandson was her pride and joy and a tight rein was to her the best way of expressing that love and concern.

Those first four years of Roy's life in Sulphur Springs were an unending struggle to survive. "I can remember there were many days when we were all hungry," says Roy. "It was a very limited existence, eked out of beans and a little fatback, with biscuits as an occasional treat, made by Uncle Bob on the wood stove."

Then one day the lure of California beckoned as it had for so many stricken families in the Dust Bowl states. Roy recalls that his uncle sat him on his knee and said: "Well, son, we're thinking about going to California and I'd like to know what you think about us going out there?" The year was 1939 and Roy Coats was four years old.

The decade that started with the crash of the stock

market, was about to end with the crash and destruction of guns and bombs. On September 1, 1939, Adolph Hitler, a feverish-eyed little man with a comical Charlie Chaplin-like moustache, announced to the world from the swastika-draped rostrum of the Knoll Opera House in Berlin that he had brought war to the world by invading Poland. Meanwhile, Japanese troops continued their rape of China. On March 28 of that year, Madrid fell before Franco's fascist troops.

At home, though, the nation was still marvelling over the World's Fair that opened in New York that spring and talking about Humphry Bogart, who came to national fame in the movie *The Petrified Forest*.

But to Bob Coats and Susie Blocker all these events were secondary to the hope of finding work in California. They set off in an old, beat-up Chevrolet truck which suffered continual mechanical breakdowns. It was fortunate that Bob Coats was a handyman with a set of tools and bits of wire or they might have gone no more than a hundred miles from home. The luckless trio stopped for a short time in Roswell, New Mexico, where the Coats family originated. Here, Roy was introduced to his Aunt Claudia, who would later become another important influence in his life.

There was something prophetic about that first ill-fated trip to California, for it was in California that Roy Coats would eventually make his success. But in 1939, California had few opportunities for yet another "Okie" family.

Of the 500,000 people who fled the Dust Bowl states during the 1930s, 300,000 of them settled in California. Californians did not take kindly to the Okies, as they became known. Newspapers of the day referred to them as hoboes or white trash, but in truth they were simply people who had dropped off the margins of a depressed economy. In the later years, these migrants would play an important part in the booming California economy. It was Will Rogers, himself a native of Oklahoma, who quipped that the Okie migration to California raised the cultural caliber of both states.

With patched tires, the body held together with bailing wire and hope, the three travellers finally nursed the old truck to the house of another Coats' brother, in the vicinity of Red Bluff in Northern California. They were just in time to witness the end of a long drought in California.

Roy, his grandmother Susie and Uncle Bob moved into

Roy — 4 years old — was given suit on way to California

a little shack. Roy's grandmother took cattle feed sacks, washed and bleached them and sewed them together to cover the cold bare floor. And slowly the bitter truth came home that there were no jobs to be had.

The rains, when they did come that year, came with a vengeance. Rivers quickly overflowed banks and the little shack became waterlogged. Roy Coats can remember the smell of cattle feed wafting up from the wet sacks on the floor. When the flood waters got to be three feet high around the shack, Uncle Bob decided enough was enough. Roy can recall his uncle picking him up and carrying him out through the water to the truck for the long ride back to Oklahoma.

Bob Coats, like so many in those days, was something of a Jack-of-all-trades. If there was work to be done, he would take a shot at it. He could cut timber, plow a field, repair fences, herd cattle, drive a truck or fix a balky combine harvester. It was this flexibility and aptitude that enabled men like Bob Coats to survive those grim years. And it was those very same qualities, passed on to the young impressionable boy, that enabled Roy Coats to overcome the considerable odds against his ultimate success. Stamina, perseverance, enormous aptitude, impeccable honesty, a belief in hands-on learning, loyalty and flexibility — a pretty rich harvest to come from an old and ailing drifter who had singlehandedly pulled himself up from the pit of alcoholism but a few years before.

That first trip to California signaled a return to the drifter's life for Bob Coats and his adopted family. On their return to Oklahoma they scraped by on a few odd jobs, but by then bigger events were unfolding which would influence their lives — and the lives of almost everyone else in America and around the world. The American economy was about to burst into life again, signaling an end to the Great Depression of the 1930s.

Gone With The Wind was breaking box office records as the year 1940 dawned. Roadside jukeboxes were playing "Oh, Johnny Oh!" The first helicopter flew for fifteen minutes and nylon stockings appeared on the nation's counters and disappeared just as quickly. The Golden Gate Bridge was completed. Joe Louis was Heavyweight Champion of the World and the Cincinnati Reds were riding high on their way to beat the Detroit Tigers in a seven-game World Series.

By and large, most Americans were enjoying a false sense of security as the European war seemed to be at a standstill following the fall of Poland. When President Roosevelt asked Congress in his State of the Union Message for $1.8 billion to finance the biggest peacetime military build-up in the history of the United States, his critics dubbed him a warmonger.

Then, as spring 1940 came, Hitler's troops overran Denmark in a few hours, Norway in a matter of days. In May, stormtroopers blitzed through Belgium, Luxembourg and Holland. Next came France — whose modernized army had been considered the best in the world. Hitler's panzers sliced through France and reached Paris almost as fast as the tanks would carry them. Italy, greedy for a share of the spoils, entered the war on the side of Germany and the two Axis powers ruthlessly set about seizing the rest of Europe in their iron grip.

In the month of May alone, German U-boats sank 75,000 tons of British shipping and, with Hitler's invasion boats lined up in French ports, American opinion made a dramatic about-face.

President Roosevelt asked and got from Congress another $4.8 billion to beef up American armaments. At that time, the U.S. Army ranked 17th in total manpower and modern weapons among the armies of the world — with less capacity than the late Polish army, which Hitler's troops had obliterated in only 27 days.

In California, the aircraft industry was given the task of boosting airplane production to an astounding 50,000 planes a year. Field Marshal Hermann Goering, the mastermind of German aviation, scoffed that it was "Unbelievable!" Within a short time airplane production in the United States shot up to an annual rate of 60,000 planes.

All this activity prompted Bob Coats to return to California with his small family. Again they met with some of the Coats' clan in Roscoe, which is now called Sun Valley, a suburban Los Angeles community between the Foothills and eastern edge of the sprawling San Fernando Valley. Bob Coats' sister, Claudia, and her husband, Joe Spencer, had left Roswell, New Mexico and bought a small house next door to Paul Coats, another of the Coats brothers. Paul Coats and his wife had a son, William Lee, nicknamed "Buzz," who in later life made a name for himself as a speed boat racer before a high speed accident ended his life prematurely.

Bob Coats managed to get a job at last and Roy's grandmother, Susie, found work at a nearby packing plant, plucking turkey feathers. During the day, Roy would play with his cousin, "Buzz," on the dry gravel washes of the Big Tujunga Wash at a place known as Horny Toad Flats. At night, Roy would help his grandmother pluck turkey feathers. For a short while, some semblance of stability and security had entered Roy's life.

The impetus to move again actually came from Washington. As war preparations mounted, word came that the federal government was going to freeze job occupations. For a free-spirited drifter like Bob Coats, this was tantamount to being sentenced to jail. Bob Coats quit his job, collected Roy and his grandmother and they were on the road again. It was the start of a rootless life that would lead them through Arizona, Texas, New Mexico and Oklahoma as Uncle Bob moved from job to job.

In Roosevelt, Texas, Uncle Bob got a temporary job cutting trees for fence posts. Roy went to the local school and found that an Okie in Texas was no more welcome than in California. The local kids lined up to pound on young Roy, but they soon found out he was not an easy mark.

From Roosevelt they moved to the town of Springer, Oklahoma and here the bullies were twin boys who took the lead in showing Roy he wasn't welcome there either. The twin boys, who were older and bigger than Roy, would both jump him.

"One would hold me on the ground while the other would pound me," Roy recalls with a laugh. "Then they'd change off and the other would pound me. I got thrashed pretty good."

But the real problem, as far as Roy was concerned, was his grandmother's inflexible rule that if he came home beaten up, he would get another whipping from her. Roy solved it in a practical fashion that revealed a growing sense of tactics. First, he made sure not to be around when the twins were together. He took to waiting and watching for them until one or the other was alone.

"Whoever came by, I'd jump on him and beat him for all he was worth. I never knew for sure which one I was beating on," Roy recalls, "because they were identical twins, but I'm pretty sure I got them both because soon they would light out if they saw me, even when they were together."

Roy would not himself become a bully through these experiences but, with his background, he realized early that if he didn't stick up for his own rights no one else would. He didn't go around with a chip on his shoulder, as perhaps he had every right to do, but his bantam scrappiness and growing skill with his fists soon had him dubbed as very precocious for his age and even a trouble-maker. In truth, it was more the growing assertion of that fierce individualism and frontier belief in sticking up for one's own rights that he inherited from his Uncle Bob.

That inheritance would show up dramatically some 27 years after his run-in with the Springer twins. In 1967, thieves stole irreplaceable machine tools and gauges from Roy's growing manufacturing company. Faced with the prospect of having to close down and losing his hard-won customers, Roy formed a vigilante posse from among his own workers to track and catch the thieves. He recovered the critical tools and gauges and kept the business running.

"Any man who won't stick up for his own rights, for whatever reason," Roy observes quietly, "must rely on someone else to enforce those rights for him, or simply give them up altogether."

3
ENDINGS AND NEW BEGINNINGS

One of the reasons Roy Coats has been so successful in business is his remarkable aptitude and innate mechanical skill. Both have been put to the test may times over the years in the course of building up 15 different companies.

Again, one finds the influence of Bob Coats on Roy. While living in Springer, Oklahoma, Bob Coats acquired an old ten-wheeler dump truck and used it to haul lime for local farmers. The young boy would ride with his uncle every chance he got. Uncle Bob would put Roy on his lap and let him help steer the truck. It was the start of a lifelong fascination with big machinery. Even today, Roy Coats never seems to be more content or more at home than when riding high in the cab of a tractor-trailer or putting a bulldozer or rock picker through its paces.

The lime-hauling business was a small step-up for the family, but not much. When winter came the lime business dropped off and the family of three would be on the move again, looking for work.

On December 7, 1941, all hopes of peace went up in the broiling clouds of smoke that covered Pearl Harbor. The industrial might of America shifted into high gear as the U.S. went to war.

The entry of America into World War II persuaded Bob Coats to overlook FDR's job freeze. He loaded Grandmother Susie and young Roy into the dump truck and set out for New Mexico, where a new Air Force base needed outside truck drivers.

Bob Coats was around sixty years old by then. The work was hard and demanding and it took all of his considerable fortitude to keep working. As a young man he had spent many years in a copper mine and his dust-weakened lungs were now developing cancer.

On those days when Bob Coats was too sick and weak to work, Roy and his grandmother would tend him, nursing him along until he was strong enough to return to work. That example of stamina and old-fashioned guts during that time in New Mexico left an indelible impression on Roy Coats.

Meanwhile, events in the world at large roared on toward their momentous and costly climax. In 1942, U.S. and Filipino troops surrendered to the Japanese on Bataan and Corregidor, but later that same spring the U.S. achieved the first of its great victories over Japanese sea power in the battles of the Coral Sea and Midway. On the other side of the world, U.S. and British troops landed in French North Africa and Field Marshal Rommel's troops were defeated in the battle of El Alamein.

In between bouts of sickness, Bob Coats labored on at the Air Force base, but in 1944, work for outside drivers slacked off and the small family was forced to return to Sulphur Springs, Oklahoma, yet again.

1944 was also the year that U.S. and British troops landed at Anzio and on June 6 the Normandy invasion began. By August 25, Paris was liberated and U.S. troops were invading the Philippines as the costly and bloody job of driving the Japanese back across the Pacific went into high gear. Bing Crosby won an Oscar that year for the movie *Going My Way*. For Bob Coats, young Roy and his grandmother, it was a year much like the ones that had gone before. Bob Coats resumed hauling lime to farmers, in between increasingly frequent bouts of illness. In the winter months, the three travelled from one itinerant job to another, moving from one rundown transient motor court to the next.

"We just sort of made our tour," recalls Roy Coats. "I'm not complaining about this," he adds quickly, "because if it did nothing else, it made me tough. I think if I had a choice of being protected until the day I walked into college, or being brought up the way I was — I'd take the rough trip every time. You not only become physically tough, you become mentally tough as well. It creates a feeling of self-reliance so that in later life people cannot ride over you. So often I find it disarms people when they can't just roll over you."

In 1945, Allied troops smashed through Hitler's defenses around Berlin and on May 1, 1945, Hitler committed suicide in his bunker. On May 7, the war in Europe was over, one month after the death of Franklin D. Roosevelt. FDR did not live to see final victory in Europe nor the fateful step into the atomic age taken that August over Hiroshima and Nagasaki by his successor, Harry S. Truman. And neither did Bob Coats.

To afford what relief they could, doctors put Bob Coats on an evil-smelling sulphurous medication. The smell was enough to turn faint stomachs, but Roy would not leave his side. Uncle Bob repeatedly told the boy to sleep with his grandmother, but Roy insisted on sleeping with him at night as he had always done.

It was not, as Roy explains today, an attempt to make a noble gesture. "I loved that man so much — he was my whole life. I wouldn't have any part of being separated from him."

With Bob Coats now in bed permanently, life became literally desperate for the small family. Susie Blocker's son, Jim Blocker, today recalls Roy and his mother hiding out in his small apartment when the rent collector came around. Finally, Bob Coats was taken to a hospital in Oklahoma City, where pain killing drugs could be administered to ease his final days.

The separation from his uncle was heart-rending for the ten-year-old boy and even today the old emotion surfaces when Roy recalls those last days of his beloved Uncle Bob.

Although Roy visited his uncle as often as he could, it was never enough for Roy. He was determined to be with his uncle to the end, but even this resolution was cruelly thwarted at the last moment. Roy's mother suddenly appeared, determined to take Roy back with her to California. His grandmother fought bitterly with her daughter, but finally her daughter won and hauled an extremely distraught and unwilling Roy with her to California.

A short time later a simple letter arrived from his grandmother. Uncle Bob was dead.

4
NEW HORIZONS

Roy Coats is fond of saying that attitude is all important. "It is so basic and simple," he says, "that whatever you are doing you do it to the very best of your ability — whether it is washing the car, playing a sport or doing your job."

Roy Coats' first venture into business is a good illustration of that attitude. With the money from Bob Coats' life insurance, Susie Blocker had just enough to make a down payment on two small duplexes on Southwest 21st Street, in Packing Town, Oklahoma City, then and now the poorest district in the city. As the name implies, Packing Town is located in the heart of the huge complex of stockyards and meat packing plants in that part of the city. On warm days you could cut the odor with a knife.

Susie Blocker set up house in one of the duplexes and rented the other to her son, Jim, a truck driver. Jim's rent was just enough to handle the mortgage payments. Roy's reunion with his mother was short-lived. Even in death, Bob Coats seemed to be reaching out to the bitterly bereaved boy to keep him close. With the change in Susie's fortunes brought about by his insurance policy, Roy's mother had a change of heart. Within months he was back with his grandmother, Susie, in the little duplex in Packing Town. But apart from the rent of the second duplex, which was needed to pay the mortgages, there was no other dependable source of income for Roy and his grandmother.

"It was nip and tuck," Roy recalls of those days. "We just sort of survived there somehow on Southwest 21st Street."

It soon became obvious to Roy that it was going to be up to him to keep things running and, at the age of eleven, he took his first step into the world of business. It was his attitude that got him a start. He presented himself to one of the concessionaires at the large sports stadium next to the

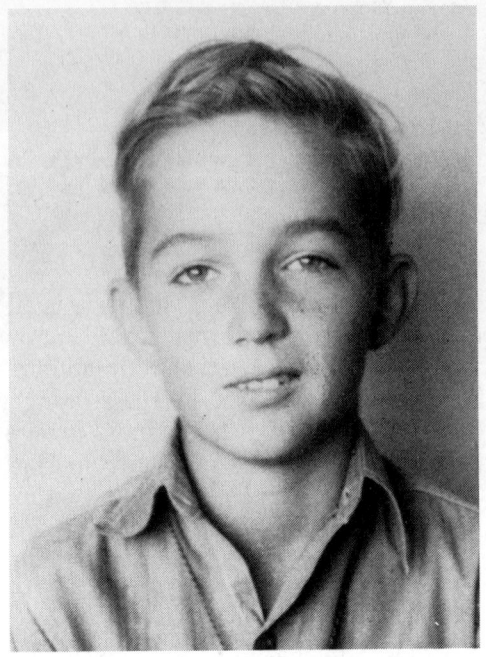

Roy at 10 working the Sterling, Illinois Gazette as newsboy

stockyards (since burned down). At first glance Roy didn't make much of an impression — a skinny, somewhat undernourished kid in old patched clothes. But his cheeks were scrubbed and the patches were neat and what he lacked in appearance he more than made up for in sheer determination. "I can work hard and run fast," he told the concessionaire. "I'll help you sell more soft-drinks."

Roy's first job was to lug cases of soft-drinks up and around the stadium for sale to the patrons. "We'll see how you work out," the concessionaire told Roy, unsure that the boy had the stamina to carry the heavy cases of drinks around the stadium hour after hour. Roy proved to be as good as his word, and the few dollars he brought into the household enabled them to survive. For the first time in his life, Roy had spending money.

In fact, the concessionaire was so impressed at the young boy's determination and drive that he made him his assistant that summer, selling drinks at the nearby ballpark. Roy now had two jobs — one selling soft-drinks during ice shows, wrestling, boxing, horse shows and livestock auctions at the stadium and another at the ballpark during the summer months. It was also the start of Roy's lifelong fascination and joy in the game of baseball.

During this time, Roy's mother drifted back to Oklahoma and went to work as a waitress at the then prestigious Marquette Hotel in downtown Oklahoma City. The job also provided her with a room in the hotel. For the first time, Roy's mother and grandmother began to mellow toward each other. Roy began to feel a little closer toward his mother, also for the first time.

Despite his disadvantaged upbringing and nights and weekends working at the stadium or ballpark, Roy somehow managed to scrape through from one school grade to the next, although no one would ever accuse him of being a good student. The only continuity he experienced in his education was the succession of bullies he fought. As a result he became a good wrestler and boxer and developed a knack for sizing up people — which he would put to good use in later life. As one of Roy's business associates says of him today: "When it comes to one-on-one handling of people in business, Roy has no peer."

Through a friend of his mother's, Roy also got a third job — selling Sunday newspapers on Saturday nights on a downtown street corner. At long last, Roy felt he was beginning to take control of his life.

Although born of necessity, his new-found entrepreneurial skills were beginning to open up new horizons. In a world that until then had shown him only the gray face of failure, the novel idea that success might be possible started to grow. It would soon become a burning desire to succeed.

Two incidents during that time stand out in Roy's memory. A gang of tough juveniles found easy pickings preying on younger, smaller newsboys. The gang would wait until the boys had sold all their papers, then move in and take the boys' hard-earned money.

After being caught and robbed three times, Roy sat down to think his way through the problem. He was determined he wasn't going to quit the job. His solution was simple but effective. He noticed the gang was so greedy they would always wait until the very last paper was sold before robbing the boys. Roy's solution was to remove small sections of the paper that wouldn't be missed and so build up what looked like another paper. He would then saunter into the lobby of the Black Hotel. To the gang watching, it appeared he had one paper left and had gone into the hotel to find a buyer, or to use the washroom. While they waited around outside, Roy would throw the dummy paper in the trash, leave smartly through the side entrance and waste no time in getting home.

The second incident had a more lasting effect, being a blow not to his pocket but to his pride. While in his own mind he was fast becoming a regular street tycoon, to others he was still an undernourished little ragamuffin. At Christmas that year, he was called into the office of a small Christian community center which ran a gymnasium for local children. He was told that he had been invited to attend a Christmas party. Never having been to a party before, he didn't think too much about it.

When the day of the party arrived, Roy was picked up — together with a local girl about his own age — and driven to the home of an affluent citizen in the north end of town. There, as he stood in a room surrounded by well-meaning adults all laden with gifts, he was told that he and the girl had been selected by a group of community-minded citizens as the neediest boy and girl in the neighborhood. Suddenly aware of the holes in his socks and the used clothing that didn't fit, Roy blushed with embarrassment mingled with total wonder at all this largesse.

"I was absolutely overwhelmed," Roy recalls today. "They showered me with new shirts and slacks, shoes, baseball gloves and a bat. I was in awe. I'd never seen anything like that in my whole life."

For many years now, Roy Coats has been something of a philanthropist in his own right, but he has never forgotten that generosity and charity can often be extremely uncomfortable to those on the receiving end. As a result, he rarely speaks of his own generosity and never makes a display of it.

Talking with Roy in his Burbank office one day during research for this book, I had occasion to witness his spontaneous generosity. A young stockroom boy had lost some of his prized possessions when his apartment was burglarized the day before. Roy had obviously overheard office gossip about it. Roy glanced up, saw the young man through the window, excused himself and went out. I watched as the Chairman of the Board quietly slipped the young man a fistful of money to help him replace his stolen possessions, just a few days before Christmas. Roy had not intended that anyone should witness the gesture. It was strictly something between the Chairman of the Board and one of his junior employees.

5
MONTANA INTERLUDE

That Christmas in Oklahoma City — with its unexpected windfall of donated gifts — marked the end of Roy's close relationship with his grandmother, Susie. He was about to experience something like the All-American home life that the majority of his contemporaries took for granted. But, typically, it was to be short-lived.

The harbinger of better times went by the unlikely name of Eakle Colliflower. Eakle had been dating Roy's mother for some months. At Christmas he gave Roy a rebuilt bicycle, which Roy prized above all the gifts he had received. Shortly after Christmas, Eakle Colliflower and Roy's mother arrived at Grandmother Susie's house and annouced they had recently been married. Roy had already taken a liking to Eakle and, when his mother said they were moving to Illinois and wanted Roy to live with them, Roy agreed.

Eakle Colliflower was a handsome, dashing man with a great sense of humor. A dapper dresser, he was something of a look-alike for the movie actor George Raft in his heyday. Eakle was also a highly skilled mechanic with the interest and patience to become a needed role model for the young boy.

"For all I had learned from my Uncle Robert," Roy muses today, "Eakle showed me many things at a different level. He was better educated than my uncle, and could have been anything he wanted to be."

The trouble was that Eakle Colliflower did not want to be anything special. The ambition which had fired him to become exceptionally well qualified as a mechanic had undergone a drastic change by the time he married Roy's mother, although it wasn't evident at first.

Eakle had served with the U.S. Army during the war and had contracted a severe case of jaundice in Europe during the bitter winter of 1944/45, when Allied troops were advanc-

Eakle Colliflower with Roy's mother

ing toward Berlin. When the war in Europe ended, Eakle was shipped to New Jersey for mustering out. On landing in the U.S. he called his wife and told her he would be home that coming weekend. The Army mustered him out two days early. Wanting to surprise his wife, Eakle didn't tell her he would be home early. Surprise her he certainly did. He arrived home to find his wife in bed with another man.

Eakle divorced his wife and began to drift around the country with no real sense of purpose. By the time he met and married Roy's mother, Eakle had glossed over the wound of betrayal with his quick and ready laughter, but the wound never really healed.

Illinois was a pleasant surprise for Roy, primarily because he found his problems with other children in school had lessened dramatically. He discovered the reason he had been the object of so much antagonism was that until this time he had been effectively dressed in rags. In Illinois, he had new clothes on his back for the first time and his new "father" had a steady job as a maintenance engineer in a local steel mill. Although by no means well off, it was a considerable step up from what Roy had so far experienced.

The world at large was busy trying to adjust to the idea of peace in 1947, and nervously watching the belligerent Russians as they re-drew the map of Europe. The future was there to read on March 4, 1947 when the Russians rejected the U.S. plan for United Nations atomic-energy control. India was freed by the British that year and both the Truman Doctrine (of military and economic assistance to nations threatened by Communism) and the Marshall Plan went into

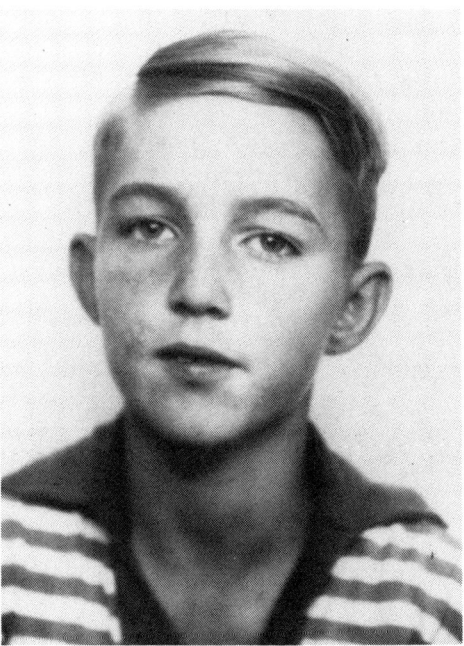

Roy — 11 years old — selling cokes and hot dogs in Oklahoma City Stadium

effect. And Roy Coats was hard at work building up his newspaper route, delivering word of this strange new world on his bicycle.

Roy revelled in the responsibilities of maintaining a paper route, making collections and turning the money over to the newspaper office each week.

"I really enjoyed that," Roy recalls. "I was never bashful about knocking on doors and saying: Hi, I'm the paper boy in the area. Would you like the *Sterling Gazette*."

As a result, the route increased in size substantially. At long last the years of drifting seemed to be over.

Perhaps things were going too well for Eakle Colliflower. The orderly life of a solid citizen seemed to weigh heavily upon him.

"I was looking over the tall trees this morning," Eakle announced one day, in true drifter tradition. "I think it's time maybe for us to move on."

For months the family drifted from one town to another, Eakle working in fits and starts, until they arrived back in Oklahoma City. It seemed like things were about to fall apart yet again when Eakle received a job offer in Billings, Montana.

The job of maintenance man in a meat packing plant didn't pay a lot, but it was just enough to afford a trailer home across the street from the plant.

Roy was enrolled at Billings Junior High and immediately set about building up a paper route for the *Billings Gazette*. Early winter mornings in Montana can be rugged in the extreme. It is not uncommon for the thermometer to reach −30 or −40 degrees. The very air cuts painfully into the mouth and lungs.

If nothing else, a morning paper route during a Montana winter builds endurance. And endure Roy did. At 40 degrees below you pump hard to get the frozen bicycle chain and bearings to move as you wobble off in the snow. You try to avoid being caught in the hard crusty ruts and hope there isn't a patch of blue or black ice lurking beneath the powder snow to send you and the bike flying. You remember stories of children who got a tongue or finger stuck to a metal post or pump handle.

But spring always came and finally summer. Roy found he had a pretty good arm for baseball. He was good at bat and even better at pitching. He began to dream of a career as a professional baseball player. He certainly had the winning attitude. Racing to a ball game on his bicycle during his twelfth year, the chain came off and Roy went flying, shattering his four front teeth on the street. Wiping away blood and bits of broken teeth, Roy put the chain back on and continued to the ballpark. He was heartbroken when the coach wouldn't let him pitch the game and sent him home.

On weekends, Eakle would patiently teach Roy how to use mechanic's tools. If nothing else, Eakle always kept their

Roy's mother

Roy is 14 and leaving Billings, Montana for California

old car in first-class running condition and eventually Roy became skilled enough to take over repair and maintenance of the car.

The four years Roy spent in Billings were the most stable years he had so far experienced. Eakle stuck with his job in the meat packing plant for two years, then the jaundice struck again. The attack was so severe that Eakle almost died. As a result, he lost the job in the packing plant and the family's hard-won gains began to slide away.

"We had a terrible time for a while," Roy remembers. "We moved into a real shack in the south end of town. My mother worked as a cook for the railroad and we were just barely scraping by. Even though our living standards had gone up a few notches from the poverty conditions of life in Sulphur Springs, Oklahoma, we were still on the wrong side of the tracks, still in the destitute end of town. And I'm not too sure, in the case of Eakle Colliflower, if that wasn't almost by choice.

He just didn't want to get involved in a style of living where there was any pressure on him to maintain a house payment or become involved in society."

Following Eakle's illness and his eventual recovery, the relationship between Eakle and Roy's mother deteriorated fast. Roy's mother was still a young woman in her late twenties and remarkably attractive. The emotional wound from Eakle's first marriage flared up again. He began to accuse Roy's mother of countless infidelities and life became a running battle, with young Roy caught in the middle. Even so, Roy managed to start the tenth grade in Billings, but that was the end of his formal education.

It was 1949 and Roy was fourteen years old. In China, the Communist People's Republic had just been proclaimed. On September 23rd that year, the Soviet Union set off its first atomic bomb. Although no one suspected it then, the United States was only ten months away from being engaged in another war, this time in a place few Americans had heard of — Korea.

Roy was now tall and lean, but no longer skinny. Summers working on local ranches had toughened him, so that he seemed far older than his years. Once again, Eakle was "looking out over the tall trees."

Roy, weary of the constant bickering between his mother and Eakle, decided enough was enough. With summer work on local ranches, which took him away from home, Roy already had a taste of independence and liked it.

He packed a small bag, slung it over his shoulder and started out for California. He was on his way to find the real father he had never known and to try his grit on the world.

6
THE OPEN ROAD

In true drifter tradition, Roy jumped a freight train heading west, but after ten miles it stopped in a yard. Roy decided to try his luck on the highway.

For all his early privations, being totally alone was a new and chastening experience.

"There is a terrible lonely feeling that develops," Roy recalls. "You begin to feel so meaningless in the whole scheme of things. People are rushing by in their cars and you're just standing there, wanting to do something, having an objective, but you're totally at the will and pleasure of the people driving by."

But it also proved to be an invaluable experience for the fourteen-year-old boy. It gave him time to think and reflect, to sort out the life he was leaving behind and clear the decks for the new life ahead. Valuable, too, were the instructive encounters with ranchers, housewives, tourists and businessmen who gave Roy rides. Many of these people opened up their lives to Roy in a way he had not previously experienced. To Roy it seemed that being a total stranger passing through their lives disarmed their normal reserve. Perhaps they would not have been so frank had they known he was only fourteen years old. As it was, these confidences gave him insights not often afforded to a youngster.

One such encounter was with a man named Nedward Frost. If you were interested in hunting and fishing in the late Forties and early Fifties, you probably subscribed to *Field and Stream* or *Argosy Magazine*. Here one could read of great hunters and guides. Preeminent among these was Nedward Frost, a legendary hunting guide and tracker in the wilds of Wyoming. Sportsmen would come from all over America to have Ned Frost guide them to trophy size bear, elk and bighorn sheep.

In the early fall of 1949, Ned Frost stopped to pick up a young boy hitchhiking on a lonely mountain road in Wyoming. The young boy was Roy Coats. Ned took a shine to the plucky teenager and offered him a job as night guard at his hunting camp, not far from Cody, Wyoming, in the Grand Teton Mountains near Yellowstone Park.

Roy's job was to stay awake and drive off any wandering bears or coyotes looking for a quick meal. The hunting party Ned was guiding at that time believed steady hard drinking was an integral part of hunting. They packed along more liquor than food and ammunition.

In all truth, Roy had not been looking forward to encountering his first bear, but the first few nights went smoothly. That is to say neither bears nor coyotes put in an appearance.

One night the hunters were celebrating with more than their usual gusto and pressured Roy to join in the fun. Roy's only exposure to alcohol at that time was the occasional sip of Eakle Colliflower's beer. That night he downed the better part of a generous bourbon and 7-Up and fell asleep on watch. As luck would have it, that was the night a small brown bear wandered into the camp to rummage around the tents.

The noise of the bear pawing its way through cans and bottles woke Roy. In the dead of night, by the flickering glow of a campfire, even a small bear can easily assume gigantic proportions to the inexperienced eye. To Roy's befuddled senses, what he thought he saw was a Grizzly.

"Bear! Bear!" he yelled at the top of his lungs, then practically ran straight up the side of the nearest tree.

The drowsy hunters were wakened by all the commotion. They shooed the bear away, then broke into laughter at the sight of the wide-eyed boy clinging to the branches of a tree.

The hunters thought it was a good joke — a night guard scared into a tree by a small brown bear — but Nedward Frost didn't share their amusement. Roy was demoted and sent back to the base camp to watch over Ned Frost's sheep.

The best sheep handlers in the world have long since learned the only way to successfully herd stubborn sheep is with the assistance of some smart dogs. Roy had only himself and a horse. Chasing after some sheep that had wandered down into a draw, Roy's horse stumbled. Roy was thrown to the ground, then the horse rolled on top of him. He was so badly bruised he couldn't get to his feet. Luckily, one of the other ranch hands rode out later to see how he was doing and found him. It was almost a week before Roy could get around by himself and, by that time, he had come to the firm realization that being a Wyoming sheepherder was not the future he had in mind. Roy said his farewells to Nedward Frost and set out again for California.

Roy headed west into the spectacular mountain ranges of Idaho. But for his stubbornness and a sixth sense for survival, he might well have gone no further.

On the outskirts of a small mountain town a car skidded to a stop and a wild-eyed man told Roy to jump in. The radio was blaring and at each stoplight on the way out of town the driver left a streak of rubber behind. By the time they were through the outskirts of the town and heading into the mountains, it was obvious to Roy the man was intoxicated. As they began to negotiate the twisting mountain road, Roy realized the man was a danger to himself and anyone else on the road. As politely as he could, Roy asked the man to stop the car and let him out.

"Why you chicken kid, what's the matter with you?" the driver replied. "We'll make it down the mountain alright!"

Again, Roy asked to be let out and again the man refused, embroidering his insults. Most fourteen-year-olds would probably have let it go at this point when faced with the unpredictable truculence of an adult, but Roy wasn't about to give up. Finally the man pulled over on the shoulder of the road, swearing at the boy. Roy grabbed his bag, jumped out of the car and watched it take off in a spray of gravel and burnt rubber.

The relief was enormous. Roy stood there for a moment, listening to the sounds of tortured tires fade away down the mountain, then sat down to wait for another ride.

A short time later an old truck pulled to a stop. It was held together with wire and bent nails. Inside was a leathery old man who seemed to be similarly held together. He was surprised to see a young boy all alone on the mountain road. Roy explained about the drunk driver and their wild ride.

Some thirty minutes later the truck rumbled around a sharp bend and came to a stop. In front of them was the crumpled remains of the car Roy had been riding in. It was a total wreck, having smashed into the mountain at a high rate of speed. Roy and the old man got out to see what they could do. The driver was dead, his blood splashed about the twisted steel and glass.

This was Roy's second brush with mortality and he didn't like it one little bit. But what hit home even more than the man's death was the fact that if he hadn't insisted on getting out when he did, Roy himself would have ended up the same way. In later years, Roy found that failure to stand by his conviction was fatal.

Roy's odyssey to California continued in fits and starts. A little further south from the scene of the accident, Roy went into a local tavern for a hamburger. Partway through his meal, the door burst open and the movie actor Forrest Tucker and his entourage roared in.

At first, Roy thought Tucker was making a complete fool of himself — hooting and hollering, ordering drinks for everyone in the place. But as he watched, Roy realized Tucker was just having a good time. Perhaps that's what success is really all about, Roy remembers thinking at the time — being able to do what you want and not really caring what other people think about you. At any rate, it was an attitude toward success that Roy certainly employed during the more boisterous early days of his own success.

Perhaps there is no such thing as coincidence, but many years after that scene in the tavern, Roy Coats found himself a member of the same club as Forrest Tucker. It would be nice to relate that Tucker remembered the young lad in that tavern but in truth, of course, he did not.

Sightseeing was not exactly what Roy had in mind when he set out for California, but the wild grandeur of Wyoming and Idaho had a lasting effect, touched that "still place in the soul" of which he had not, until that time, been aware. It also fostered a growing interest and pride in the heritage of the land and the people with courage enough to venture across it to form a nation. It was, so to speak, an education of the senses.

Even today, Roy feels fortunate that as a boy he was exposed to such experiences. Preeminent in his memory, though, is his first sight of the awesome grandeur of the Grand Canyon. A detour to northwestern Arizona had not been·part of Roy's plan, but a tourist offered to drive him close to the Arizona-California border if he would first accompany the tourist on a tour of the Grand Canyon. Roy agreed, thinking it would be no trouble at all to catch a final ride to his destination.

The approach to the Canyon does little to prepare the visitor for what lies ahead, although one can sense the presence of the Grand Canyon, in much the same way one senses the presence of an ocean just over the horizon.

Nothing in Roy's past experience or education had prepared him for that mile deep chasm in the interior of the earth's crust. It is as though nature had taken off all restraint, casually laying open hundreds of millions of years of evolution for all to see. Vermillion colored cliffs, stone rainbows, purple depths, precipices, buttes, slopes, spires and temples of rock in red, gold, pink, green, orange and mauve, all carved by millions of years of patient erosion by the Colorado River.

For some people it can be an unnerving experience to look down into the Canyon, making one's life and efforts seem insignificant compared to the enormous span of geological time in which mankind is but a very recent phenomenon. For Roy Coats it was a joyous and freeing experience — like a fresh breeze catching the sail of his imagination.

On leaving the Grand Canyon, the tourist stopped to make a telephone call to his home. Reluctantly, he told Roy he could not carry out his promise to drive him to the California border as he had to return immediately to Colorado. The wilderness surrounding the Canyon is no place to try and hitch a ride. Roy swallowed his disappointment and accompanied the tourist back into Colorado.

The tourist let Roy off in the town of Montrose, almost six thousand feet above sea level in the middle of Colorado mountain country. In the mountains, fall was rapidly becoming winter. Roy soon realized there was no way he could stand out on the highway in freezing temperatures, dressed as he was in thin summer clothes.

Wandering through Montrose, Roy saw a sign advertising an opening for a ranch hand. The next day he was hired on at the John Beach Ranch in Ridgeway, twenty miles south of Montrose. Roy, of course, lied about his true age.

The routine at the ranch was simple but demanding. Up at four in the morning to milk cows, then a big ranch-style breakfast with the family before taking feed to cattle in the mountain pastures. Hard work even in good weather but when temperatures drop below freezing the bales of hay become frozen stiff. Loading bales from the hay loft to a wagon under these conditions is taxing work, to say the least. When the wagon was loaded, Roy's job was to pitch the bales from the wagon as it was pulled across the pasture by a jeep.

Roy was not found wanting in his work and no one suspected he was only fourteen. Jack Beach, the eighteen-year-old son of the owner, treated Roy as his equal at all times, assuming Roy to be of his own age and interests. Consequently, when work was finished, Jack would drive Roy into Ridgeway with him to play pool, drink beer and socialize with Jack's friends, both male and female.

The only problem was that Jack Beach was newly married and had an infant son. Jack's father didn't take kindly to his son continuing to play the free and easy bachelor life. Unfortunately, he came to the totally wrong conclusion that it was Roy who was leading his son astray. It was the dead of winter when Jack Beach's father took Roy aside and told him he could no longer afford to keep Roy on at the ranch, pointing out that the next ranch down the line had a lot of cattle and could probably afford to take him on.

"I knew he was trying to get rid of me, but I could see no point in arguing with him," says Roy. "I figured if he didn't want me around, what else could I do?"

Roy was driven down the line to the next ranch and hired, but his luck had temporarily run out. Instead of a warm private bunkhouse to sleep in, Roy was led up a ladder to the cold attic of the ranch house to bed down. Instead of good wholesome food, every meal was swimming in grease that boiled his stomach.

"I remember the owner telling me that as the pumpkins and squash he kept in the attic didn't freeze, he didn't expect I would either.

"It was a downhill slide from the very beginning. The ranch had three to four times the number of cattle as the Beach Ranch.

"We'd be out there in the cold until I was just about frozen to death," Roy remembers. "The owner wasn't much of a worker either, so I ended up doing the bulk of the work."

Roy stuck it out until he had saved twenty dollars, then quit, determined to hitchhike his way to California, winter or not. His first stop was the small town of Ouray, at the north end of the Red Mountain Pass. Roy wanted to say goodbye to one of the girls he had become friendly with during his visits to town with Jack Beach.

It was snowing the day he left the ranch for Ouray. By the time he reached town, a full-blown mountain snowstorm was in progress. There was no hope now of catching a ride through the pass to Silverton and down into Durango and the New Mexico border beyond.

The girl Roy had come to see worked in a local restaurant. She was happy to see him. When Roy explained his situation, she introduced him to the owner of the restaurant. A deal was worked out that if Roy would clean up around the restaurant his meals would be free.

That night, Roy rented a small room fully expecting to be on his way the next day. The snow continued to fall the next day and the day after that. Within a few days his twenty dollars had run out and the roads out of Ouray were still blocked in all directions. In desperation, Roy walked into the local sheriff's office and tried to convince the sheriff to let him sleep in one of the empty cells. The sheriff firmly showed Roy the street.

Without money, Roy's only alternative was to walk the streets to keep himself from freezing to death. When evening came he knew he had to do something. The young girl was the only person he knew in town, so he summoned up his nerve and knocked on the door of her house. To his surprise and then relief, the girl's father answered the door and welcomed Roy into the warm house. He insisted that Roy join them for supper.

Later, Roy realized it would have been better had he been totally honest with the family and explained his plight right at the beginning, but his pride wouldn't let him admit he was desperate and penniless. Instead, he kept the conversation going until the girl's parents finally excused themselves and went to bed. When the girl herself went to bed, Roy curled up on the floor by the wood stove and went to sleep.

Although surprised to see Roy the next morning, the girl's father hospitably offered Roy breakfast before leaving for work. His surprise turned to slight annoyance when Roy showed up the next night to repeat the performance. By the third night his patience had come to an end. He threatened to call the sheriff and have Roy thrown in jail if he didn't leave the house. Roy just sat there, trying to bluff it out. He knew the sheriff didn't want to have him in his jail. Finally the girl interceded. She pleaded with her father to let Roy stay until the storm had passed and roads were clear. Faced with his daughter's anguish and Roy's stubbornness, he relented.

As soon as the storm had passed and the roads were clear, Roy said a wistful goodbye to the girl and her relieved family and hitched a ride down into Silverton. Rides in quick succession took him south into the warmer climates of New Mexico. Here, Roy heard that a new drilling rig was looking for roughnecks. He didn't want to turn up in California without a penny, so decided to try his luck in the oil fields.

By now Roy was perfecting his hitchhiking technique. Instead of waiting by the side of the road, he would go into a restaurant near the highway and observe the people inside. When he overheard someone mention they were driving in the direction he wanted to go, Roy would strike up a conversation and gradually steer the talk around to his own destination of California. Invariably he was offered a ride. He was learning how to observe and size up people — skills that would prove invaluable in later years.

It was during one such conversation that Roy heard of the opening for roughnecks. He ended up in a car with two young Texans on their way to what was then the middle of nowhere — the new oil boom town of Farmington, New Mexico. Again, Roy lied about his age and all three were signed on by the Great Western Drilling Company as roughnecks — a very descriptive word for the hard slogging work on a drill platform.

They worked day and night for two weeks, racking up all the overtime they could manage, oblivious of the weather. At the end of two weeks the crews were paid. Typically, the cards and dice came out on pay night. Roy drifted around the edges of the games for a while, picking up pointers, before agreeing to join in a game of Blackjack. A few hours later he pulled out of the game with five hundred dollars in his pocket — more money than he'd seen in his whole lifetime.

"For most of those roughnecks, five hundred dollars wasn't a great deal of money," Roy shrugs. "But there were some there who would cut your throat for five hundred."

When his two Texan friends told Roy later that night they had had enough of roughnecking and were heading back to Texas, Roy gratefully went with them. They parted company on old Route 66, the Texans heading due east and Roy heading due west. Within a couple of days, Roy was finally in Los Angeles.

Hot, dusty and tired, but aglow with the thought of the grubstake in his pocket, Roy made his way to Roscoe, now known as Sun Valley, and knocked on the door of his Aunt Claudia's house. Claudia was a sister of Bob Coats and Roy's father, Eugene. Roy was in high spirits and looking forward to showing his father how independent and resourceful he was to have hitchhiked all the way from Montana and arrive with five hundred dollars in his pocket.

"Land's sakes — it's little Roy!" Claudia exclaimed with delight on opening the door. She kissed and hugged him, tears in her eyes, and brought him inside. When the initial surprise was over, Roy asked about his father. Claudia's bright blue eyes clouded over.

"Roy honey, your dad's been dead two years now," she said sadly. "Him and some friend had been drinking and then they went out for a drive. Your father's friend crossed over the highway and they hit a Greyhound bus head on. They both died right at the spot."

It seemed a cruel twist of fate that after all Roy had been through, his father had been dead for two years and he didn't even know it.

"Although I heard quite a bit about him from my Aunt Claudia and Uncle Paul, I would have liked to have known him myself," says Roy wistfully.

It may seem unusual that Roy would still be able to express interest and concern for a father he never knew — a father who had deserted him before he was born and not bothered to inquire after him. But even at the tender age of fourteen, Roy had the very mature understanding that the vicissitudes and trials of a hard, impoverished life can drive people to actions they would not normally consider. At first hand Roy had seen what grinding poverty can do to decent people, let alone those with weaknesses.

That quality of nonvindictiveness has not lessened with the years or the hard trials of business. It is one of the qualities about Roy Coats that make him appear to be an enigma, even to people who are close to him.

This facility to take blows and turn them to his advantage is well illustrated by Roy's remark that the death of his father simply "strengthened my resolve to make something of myself."

At Aunt Claudia's, then, Roy found a second home. She welcomed him into her house and treated him like a long-lost son, cementing a bond of friendship and love between the two that was unshakeable. California opened up a whole new vista for Roy. He was truly on his own, independent and willing to work hard. And in California, as many before and since have discovered, there is opportunity for those who can recognize and seize upon it.

7
A NATURAL BORN SALESMAN

Stamina, perseverance, integrity, resourcefulness and the desire and capability to work harder than most — these qualities Roy Coats had demonstrated in abundance before he was fifteen years old. Qualities he had observed, absorbed and made his own over the hard years with Bob Coats and his grandmother, Susie, the years with Eakle Colliflower and during his trek from Billings, Montana to California.

What Roy would now be exposed to was the example of a truly natural born salesman — a dreamer and visionary with a steadfast belief in the power of mind over body. His name was Ernest Baum and he would leave a mark on Roy Coats that Roy readily acknowledges and is grateful for to this day.

Roy's introduction to Ernest Baum came through his cousin, William Lee (Buzz) Coats, who was exercising horses for Baum at Baum's Shadow Hills ranch, a short ride from Aunt Claudia's house in Sun Valley. Roy went with Buzz one day, met Ernest Baum and told him he was looking for work.

Today, at the age of 85 years, Ernest Baum well remembers the day Roy came to work for him. Gnarled and wiry, tough in body and words, Baum is still active around his Iron Horse Resort in Grove, Oklahoma, beside the Grand Lake of the Cherokees near the Arkansas/Missouri border.

"Roy was about fifteen then," Baum recalls. "He said he wanted a job. I remembered myself that as a boy I'd always hated to do things like pull weeds or tend sprouts, so I set him to pulling weeds along my property. Roy said 'Fine,' grabbed the tools and off he went to work. Then it seemed not any time at all had passed and he came back looking for more work. I looked around and sure enough he'd done the job.

"So I gave him some more dirty work to do," adds Baum with a smile. "And he did that, too. It seemed everything I'd give him to do, he'd do it right. I could see that here was a boy who had a desire to do something with himself. He learned very easy and had the knack of having people like him."

Even today, Baum admits he is still a hard man to work for. The young men and boys who come to his resort looking for work get the same treatment Roy Coats received over thirty years ago.

"I tell them I'm hard to work for," says Baum, "and they work harder because of that. When they do something right, though, I tell them 'Good job. You handled that the right way.' They get to thinking that if they can satify Baum, they can satisfy anybody. And that's a good thing for a boy to know."

Roy went to work for Baum doing odd jobs, grooming and exercising the horses and cleaning out the stalls. Baum's wife, Margarite, took a liking to Roy and began to treat him like her own son. Soon Roy was invited to move in with the Baums so that he wouldn't have so far to travel to work. The deal was that Baum would take Roy on as a kind of apprentice, but since he would be getting room and board as well as training he would no longer be paid a regular wage. At the time this sounded fair, but later was the cause of a temporary rift between Roy and Ernest Baum.

It was 1950 — the start of a new and perilous decade. The new age of Cold War anxiety had begun the previous summer when Russia exploded its first atomic bomb. Ahead lay the Communist invasion of South Korea. By June of that year, the United States would once again be at war. America was also about to enter the era of Senator McCarthy's rabid anti-communism campaign and the much longer era of Dwight Eisenhower as President. It was a time of new heroes, of new fears, but also a time of great expectation. The tremendous baby boom following the end of World War II fueled an unprecedented expansion as people moved from the cities to the new suburbs. Commuting came into its own, along with weekend barbecues, babysitting and a new social ritual — the cocktail party circuit.

But Roy Coats had little time to think about what was going on at large. Amid the gently rolling foothills at the edge of the San Fernando Valley, Roy was wholly engaged in the energetic, enthusiastic, hard-working but never boring world of Ernest Baum.

When Ernest Baum came to California in 1924, the first

thing he did was purchase a horse. He kept it in a stable near Griffith Park and played polo with Walt Disney and other movie pioneers of the day. Baum's real interest, though, was and is in American Saddlebred horses, prime examples of which routinely fetch fifty to one hundred thousand dollars. Over the years since then, Baum's horses have won hundreds of ribbons at shows around the country. And he is still at it, with twelve horses at his Iron Horse Resort in Oklahoma and others being trained in Missouri, Kentucky, and California.

Shortly after Roy Coats came to stay at Baum's ranch, Baum went into the manufacture of custom horse vans. He had been watching a man load some of his horses into an old truck that was overdue for the scrapyard. In those days, most horse trailers were simply converted trucks or old furniture vans with doors cut into the side. Baum looked at the old truck and said to himself: "There's got to be a better way to do this." That day he sat down and began to sketch designs for a horse van.

Baum and Roy built the first horse van in the yard. It sold right away. They built five more and they were sold. For the next 18 months, Roy was a very busy young man as Baum moved into the horse hauling business in a big way. Baum taught Roy how to drive a truck and Roy falsified his driver's application to show his age as eighteen. Barely fifteen years old, he had a chauffeur's license and was soon hauling horses in a semi-truck and trailer rig all over the Western United States.

"I admit it," says Roy today. "I was damn proud to be able to handle the big rig and be responsible for hiring a second driver as business improved."

And what better training for a young man who would himself become an entrepreneur than to be in on the ground floor with a man like Ernest Baum. Eventually, Baum's horse hauling business would expand to the point where he had Interstate Commerce permits for 46 states, in partnership with the well-known movie actor, Dale Robertson.

At fifteen, Roy shared the sweat and dream of a far from ordinary man, then in his fifties. And — most valuable of all — watched as Baum turned his dream into reality through hard work and superb salesmanship. Thirty years later, Roy can still remember how Ernest Baum taught him to be a salesman.

"Mister Baum would walk up to a horse owner and start out by admiring the man's horses," Roy recalls. "Or perhaps he would make a small joke to break down the man's resistance. Soon they would be talking together and Mister Baum would just happen to point out the smart new horse van sitting by the paddock. He would then steer the conversation around to the care and grooming of horses so that the horse owner would start thinking his way.

"Before long, the owner would find himself in total agreement with Baum's viewpoint: that a man who loved horses as much as he obviously did would only want to ship them in a modern van that met his very high standards."

From Baum, Roy also learned the value of word-of-mouth advertising — referral sales that only occur when customers are satisfied. It would be through such referral sales that Roy would build his first business. One of Roy's favorite business maxims stems from Baum — that "no deal is a good deal unless it is good for both parties concerned."

Perseverance and thorough investigation of any situation were two additional traits that Baum passed along to Roy. They would also prove invaluable in the future.

A case in point was Ernest Baum's reaction when one of his driver's lost control and a truck-load of horses overturned on the highway. None of the horses was seriously injured, but the owner filed a large lawsuit against Baum. Given the circumstances, most men would have tried to settle the claim, or simply wait for the lawyers and courts to have their way. But not Ernest Baum.

As the weeks went by following the accident, Baum made a point of checking into the horses. The owner continued to race them and Baum accumulated evidence to show that the horses ran faster and won more prize money than they had before the accident. The judge threw the case out of court.

Meanwhile, Roy was earning his stripes as a truckdriver. In those days, one of the most dangerous spots for drivers was the Grapevine — where old Highway 99 (now Interstate 5) came snaking down the steep mountain grade into the San Fernando Valley. Before today's four-lane freeway, truck accidents were a common occurrence as they lost brakes or tires on the steep, narrow, twisting downhill grade.

Roy was driving down the Grapevine one day with Ernest Baum as his passenger. The brakes failed. They had the option of staying with the truck or jumping out before the runaway's speed would make jumping impossible. Roy elected to stay with the truck and told Baum to jump.

"Good luck, boy," said Baum, and jumped.

"To this day," muses Roy, "I still believe that to jump out of that truck at that speed took far more guts than it did for me to ride it down."

Fortunately, Roy saved the truck and himself and Baum got away with a lot of bruises and some very painful scrapes.

Roy's action in staying with the truck is an interesting contrast to his earlier decision to get out of the drunk's car in Idaho, thereby saving his own life. Roy's decision to stay with the runaway truck illustrates his growing confidence in himself when he was in control of a situation. It may be stretching a point to say that Roy Coats distrusts being under the control of others and only trusts himself, but his career does tend to bear this out: he likes to drive himself, not be driven; likes to pilot a plane himself, not be a passenger; has steadfastly maintained control over major decisions in his companies, distrusting the "group think" of management committees. All of which is consistent with the classic mold of the self-made American.

The point should also be made that Roy's obvious courage was not courage without fear, but courage despite fear. Ernest Baum recalls another incident when Roy was behind the wheel of a vanload of horses that was caught in a snow blizzard on a mountain road. Baum told Roy to pull over so that he could drive. Roy looked across at Baum and said: "Don't you think I can handle it?" and kept on driving.

"I was so damn scared," Roy recalls today, "you wouldn't believe it. Cars were skidding and sliding around all over the place; sometimes you could hardly see ten feet in front of the cab, but I just kept going."

"That boy had real spunk," Ernest Baum remembers today. "He was as good a driver as any man I ever had."

Roy made another life-long friend while working for Ernest Baum. Roy had been tinkering with a 1939 Mercury, trying to get it running. One day, Jim Kaufman a regular visitor to the ranch, saw the trouble Roy was having. At the time Kaufman was a highly successful automobile dealer. The next day, Kaufman sent one of his tow trucks to the ranch and took the car to his dealership. Kaufman put in a new engine, clutch and brakes and wouldn't accept a dollar for his trouble.

That was the start of a friendship that lasted until Kaufman died two years ago. After retirement and until his death, Jim Kaufman was manager of Roy's 1800 acre Rainbow Ranch near Paso Robles.

Ernest Baum and his wife were staunch Christian Scientists and Margaret Baum decided to take Roy's, so far neglected, spiritual education in hand. While Roy did not become a Christian Scientist, despite the urging of the Baums he did attend services with them. What most impressed Roy was the Christian Scientist belief in the power of mind over body.

Although initially Roy went to the services more to please Margaret Baum than any personal desire, the experience fostered in him a sincere belief in positive thinking which has remained with him to this day. Indeed, his attitude that he would succeed despite any and all odds possibly accounts more than any other single factor for his success.

Roy stayed with Ernest Baum until he was sixteen-and-a-half years old. He was already mature for his age when he started with Baum. Now, 19 months later, Roy wanted more freedom than was available as an unofficial "member of the family." He also wanted a regular wage, and resented having to ask Baum for pocket money.

This resentment blew up one day into a heated argument with Ernest Baum. Roy went for a drive to cool down his temper. In nearby Burbank, a few miles from the ranch, he saw a Marine Corps recruiting poster. On sheer impulse he stalked into the office and signed up, using his phony driver's license to prove he was eighteen.

Later that day Roy went back to the ranch. By now he realized he might have been a trifle hasty, but figured the Marine Corps would soon find out he was under-age and forget about him.

Some days later, a Marine sergeant drove onto the ranch and asked for Roy. The sergeant had Roy's travel orders. On May 27th, 1952 Roy was inducted into the United States Marine Corps and sent to boot camp at San Diego's Marine Corps Recruiting Depot. Both Roy and the Corps had a challenge on their hands.

8
SEMPER FI AND AUNT CLAUDIA

The Korean War began June 25, 1950, when over 60,000 Soviet-equipped and controlled North Korean troops crossed the 38th parallel into South Korea, then under U.S. jurisdiction. They swiftly captured most of the South Korean peninsula. President Truman committed U.S. military and navel units to battle. Under command of General Douglas MacArthur, United States, South Korea and other United Nations troops pushed the invaders back across the border. In November that year, some 200,000 bugle-blowing Chinese troops came swarming down from bases in Manchuria and threw back the U.N. forces. Bitter fighting along the 38th parallel continued through 1951 and 1952, despite the initiation of truce talks in June 1951.

At home that year of 1951, Norman Mailer's book, *From Here to Eternity*, rocketed to the top of the best-seller lists and the cocktail circuit was abuzz with the talk of Vance Packard's book, *The Status Seekers* — a scathing and generalized attack on ambitious businessmen. Michigan romped over California in the Rose Bowl that year and the Yankees took the World Series.

For Roy Coats, Marine Corps boot camp was proving to be a severe reality adjustment as the Corps initiated him into its own concept of discipline.

"I want you to know, the Corps had to work overtime to get my devoted attention," Roy admits with a smile. "I was not about to give up my independence without a fight."

The Marine Corps had its own time-tested way of dealing with tough, street-wise young men, to whom discipline is a dirty word. "A belt in the mouth works wonders," Roy recalls, hastening to point out that he had asked for it. "Then there is guard duty instead of liberty," Roy adds, "and finally I accepted the fact they were not going to do it my way. I began to recognize that the hard work we went through every day made me feel good. I started putting some meat on my bones for the first time in my life."

At the time of his induction, Roy was sixteen-and-a-half years old, stood six-feet-two-inches but weighed a scant 155 pounds. Eleven weeks later, he had filled out to 170 pounds — all of it new muscle.

"Most of the guys in 416 platoon felt the way I did — proud to make it," Roy adds. "I saw the result of discipline and the planned exercise on myself and others. It worked. It produced a team."

In the Corps, Roy discovered that discipline is the core of application and achievement. The "Gung-ho" attitude that the Corps fosters went well with Roy's belief and positive thinking. It was an attitude that stood him in good stead when, a few years later, he decided to build his own business empire.

After eleven weeks of basic training, Roy's platoon was sent for advanced combat training and cold weather exercises to Camp Pendleton. On completion of that training, orders were given to ship the platoon for active duty in Korea.

The Korean War was an intensely savage struggle. Thousands of U.S. troops died for a few square yards of hilltop in engagements such as Pork Chop Hill and Heartbreak Ridge. American forces suffered 33,629 killed in battle and 103,284 wounded. When Red China entered the conflict, the situation became so critical that General MacArthur began to publicly advocate attacks on Chinese bases. Both the United States' and United Nations' authorities, on the other hand, were adamant in their opposition to any extension of the conflict and President Truman finally relieved MacArthur of his command.

It was with this backdrop that Roy casually announced to his Aunt Claudia, during embarkation leave, that he was soon to ship out to Korea. Aunt Claudia, who by now regarded Roy as she would her own son, was furious. The Marine Corps might be a fine place for a young man to grow up and learn discipline, she told him, but she wasn't going to stand by and see her own sixteen-year-old nephew "sent to die in some godforsaken place called Korea!"

The argument raged until Roy returned to his unit. A few days before shipping out, Roy was pulled from his platoon and advised that the Corps had received information that he was only sixteen. He was given the option of leaving the USMC or being assigned to Stateside duty. Despite his pleas to stay with his unit, the Corps could make no other decision. In the belief that when he reached eighteen he would probably be drafted anyway, Roy elected to accept Stateside duty in the corps and was sent to radio and telegraph operators school in San Diego.

It was a low period for Roy. He felt betrayed by his Aunt Claudia and emotionally torn at having to leave the platoon he had been a part of since his induction.

"To this day I don't know if I should have been angry as I was at Aunt Claudia, or thank her," Roy admits, "because a couple of years later I found that only twelve men from my platoon of sixty-eight returned from Korea."

Still seething with resentment over what had happened, Roy was not a good student at the radio/telegraph operators school. Fresh from combat training, he didn't like the prevailing attitude of some of his superiors, who wanted nothing better than to enjoy the safety and "easy duty" at the school.

To make things worse, his footlocker was stolen. Then the California Highway Patrol stopped him and issued a two-page citation for equipment violations on his car. That weekend, Roy went to Aunt Claudia's house on a two-day pass. When the two-day pass was up, Roy didn't return to San Diego.

Roy admits that never before, or since, has he felt so low and dispirited. "I felt like a traitor to the Corps," Roy recalls, "and suddenly I had no idea where my life was going."

The shame of hiding out in his aunt's house got to be too much for him. He returned to San Diego and turned himself in to the guard. He had been AWOL (Absent Without Leave) long enough to warrant a General Court Martial and was sentenced to four months in the USMC brig. It was a far-from-pleasant experience, but it did allow him to pay fully for his mistake. In time, he began to recover his sense of purpose and self-respect.

Roy during his 3 years with United States Marines

Today, Roy Coats looks back over that four months in the Marine brig as a positive experience. He met men from all walks of life and from all parts of the country. Some, like Roy, were in the brig on simple AWOL charges, while others had committed crimes ranging from theft all the way to murder. Listening to these men talk of their lives, Roy was able to sort out some of his own mixed feelings and beliefs. The confinement in the brig pushed him toward a re-examination of his values and priorities.

One of the priorities he settled on was education. He began to study in the brig and completed his high school education, receiving an equivalency diploma from the Governor of Montana. And, like many another military man who has come up against the sharp edge of military discipline, he suddenly developed an interest in the Military Code. By the time he left the brig he could argue fine points with the best of the "barrack lawyers."

Actually, one of Roy's platoon members was instrumental in rekindling his interest in education. During basic training, Pat Conway — later to become the star of the television series "Tombstone Territory" — was a member of Roy's 416 platoon. Conway deeply impressed Roy with his effective use of language. Conway always seemed to have the right word and to make himself understandable with the precision and clarity of his language.

Roy reasoned that the ability to communicate effectively would be essential for future success, regardless of what field he might enter. He set about building his vocabulary and improving his knowledge of English grammar and composition.

On discharge from the brig, Roy was re-assigned as a telephone lineman and installer. Piece by piece, the skills he would need for success were falling into place. But he was also proving to be adept at less salutory skills such as poker, craps and two-fisted drinking.

Roy became so successful at gambling that he was barred from games in his own barracks. He had to wander around the camp to find games where his reputation was not known. In one game of craps he walked off with over five thousand dollars in cash and the pink slips to a new Chevrolet and a two-year-old Ford. These were easy-come, easy-go days. The money he won would soon be spent in other games or on lavish and boisterous weekends with his Corps friends.

Roy made two close friends during this time, and both have remained friends to this day. One was Clarence (Giggles) Gilges from Conway Springs, Kansas, who now owns the local telephone company in Conway Springs. He had been a sergeant at one time, but had been demoted to corporal, following what Roy calls "a run-in with the system." The other was Lyle (Curly) Kirlin, from St. Joe, Missouri.

Whereas Clarence Gilges came from a stable family background, growing up and going to school in the same small town, Curly Kirlin's background was more or less comparable to Roy's. Roy's initial introduction to Curly was far from friendly. During an early morning march to the range for routine qualifying with the rifle, the marine directly behind Roy kept stepping on Roy's feet and legs.

"He was walking on me more than he was on the ground," Roy remembers. When time came for the men to line up again for the return march, Roy confronted the man who had been stepping all over his feet. In a few choice words, Roy explained that if on the march back to base he continued to walk over his feet, Roy would teach him a lesson. "Curly just laughed at me," Roy recalls, "and later I was awfully glad he did. He had one hell of a punch."

When they arrived back at the base, Curly said to Roy that he seemed an extremely testy individual. Roy — who admits to being more than a little cocky in those days — growled at Curly: "You're lucky you didn't walk on my feet you overgrown ass." Again, Curly simply laughed at Roy. Before long they were both laughing over the incident, and were close friends from that day on.

That cocky attitude and readiness to use his fists was partly the result of having to defend himself constantly as a child, but it was also an image encouraged by the Marine Corps in those days. "At that time, the Marine Corps had a way of making you feel you're a little bit better than you are, and willing to test it at any time," Roy explains.

As a result, Roy and his friends had more than their share of bar fights. "I was not stepping away from many people at that time," says Roy. "We were apt to take on ten as one or two. It was not too smart, but somehow we got away with it. I think back now and probably it was really foolhardy, but at the time it seemed like the thing to do. Most of the time, though, people didn't mess with us. If they did, it usually

Lyle Kirlin, Roy's Marine buddy with his wife Cindy at Rainbow Ranch

ended very quickly. Curly had a punch like a brickbat. He'd deck somebody so quickly they'd be out on the floor. When somebody hits the deck down and out before anyone else moves, it usually stops the fight right there."

Roy gained even more respect for Curly's punching ability in a bar near the small town of Hemet, about 40 miles north east of Camp Pendleton. Roy and Curly were drinking beer at a horseshoe-shaped bar. Almost directly across from Roy was a giant of a man.

"He was close to seven feet tall and had the biggest shoulders I'd ever seen in my life," says Roy. "I couldn't keep my eyes off him." When Roy went outside to the washroom, he was jumped by the big man and several of his friends. Apparently, the big man had misinterpreted Roy's interest.

"His friends held on to me," Roy recalls, "so the big guy could straighten me out. At that moment, Curly sort of danced out through the door, laid one on the big guy's chin and he was down and out before anyone could move. The others just backed off. I said to Curly, 'Come on, we'd better get out of here before that big monster wakes up.' And we did."

That wild streak in Roy would persist long after he was discharged from the Marine Corps, although he was careful to keep it under control when it came to business. Nevertheless, his drinking and rough and tumble ways were something of an enigma to his friends for many years. They found it hard to reconcile the successful, dynamic businessman they knew with the tough wild streak that lay just beneath the surface. But the genesis of that wildness can be found in his early upbringing and his experiences in the Marine Corps. When focused on business, however, that tough wild streak played a part in Roy's eventual success.

It was also during this time in the Marine Corps that the bond between Roy and his Aunt Claudia was reaffirmed. The temporary rift between them, caused by her refusal to let Roy go to Korea, was soon healed. During Roy's last year in the Corps, his liberties were usually spent at Aunt Claudia's house in Sun Valley.

"She was a lot of things to me," says Roy. "She was just a very, very wonderful person and if she liked you, you could do no wrong. You could be the worst person in town, but she would justify a relationship simply because she liked you. That's all that mattered to her. She was 100% on my side. You find a lot of people in life that will vacillate, but she wasn't one of those. She was on your side come hell or high water. I just had a tremendous amount of respect for that," Roy adds.

Aunt Claudia was similar in nature to her brother, Bob Coats, who had looked after Roy the first ten years of his life. She, too, was extremely honest and something of a holdover from earlier pioneer days. Thin, wiry and tough, she used to boast she could lick any one of her twelve brothers, if not two. She never hid or suppressed her emotions. They were there on the surface for all to see. Quick to anger, she was just as quickly placated by a kind word or gesture. Although she could, on occasion, out-yell or out-cuss any Marine, it wasn't enough to conceal a heart as big as the frontier she was raised on. Her dark blue eyes flashed and sparkled in a face that was weathered by the sun and wind of the New Mexico plains. She dressed in the style of the 1930s — simple, shapeless, cotton print dresses and plain, no-

Aunt Claudia with 5 of her 12 brothers, including Roy's father (2nd from left) and Uncle Richard (3rd from left)

nonsense button-down shoes. On the rare occasion she used makeup, it generally consisted of a quick slash of lipstick that might or might not land in the general area of her lips.

For Aunt Claudia, Roy was a great deal more than her nephew. He came to represent the children she never had. "She was proud of me and I was proud of her. She just had a magic about her," Roy recalls fondly. "We had this special love and the way we showed our love was to pick on each other incessantly."

Even in public, Aunt Claudia took delight in calling Roy "You little bastard!" It was never said with any malice behind it whatsoever, but others would often misinterpret their relationship. Roy recalls that some of his Corps friends were shocked when they first heard Aunt Claudia refer to Roy in this way and couldn't understand why Roy kept smiling.

"I told them, you don't understand... Aunt Claudia just paid me a great compliment. She doesn't know that little bastards are the best people in the world."

The very real camaraderie between Roy and Aunt Claudia was often misinterpreted by others. They did not realize that what lay behind the outer bickering and teasing was a genuine love and respect for each other.

"Some of my friends told me I was too tough on her — picking on her too much," Roy recalls. "I began to believe that perhaps I was. When I got back to base, I decided I wouldn't go to Aunt Claudia's that coming weekend. About Tuesday following the weekend I got a card from her. It said: 'What's the matter, you little bastard, don't you love me anymore?'"

Roy well understood that Claudia's tough background had not disposed her to outward displays of affection. "But she always gave me a hug and loved for me to give her a hug and a kiss. I'd stroke her wrinkled face," Roy recalls with a smile, "and tell her how beautiful she was. 'You little bastard,' she'd say, 'you better quit that!'"

As had been the case with his Uncle Bob, Roy found he could rely totally on Aunt Claudia. "She knew damn well if she called me from Arkansas and really needed me, that I'd be there just as quickly as I could get on the road or on a plane," Roy says. "And likewise, if I called her she would have been on the road in a minute. You don't have too many people in your life that you can depend on to that degree."

Aunt Claudia also functioned as Roy's bank during his time in the service. "By the time I got my paycheck on the 1st and 15th of the month, I owed most of it to Aunt Claudia," Roy remembers. "When I won money shooting dice, I'd take it to Aunt Claudia and borrow it back from her. She'd grouse like hell about that, even though it was my own money. We just had so much fun teasing each other...half the time it was hard to figure out who was putting who on."

When asked where I was going on liberty, and Roy said to his Aunt Claudia's, the normal reaction of friends who didn't know Aunt Claudia was "Oh boy, some big deal!" Once they had been to Aunt Claudia's, though, they wanted to go with Roy every chance they got.

Aunt Claudia not only made Roy and his friends feel very welcome, but somehow managed to make them feel they had always known her. There was also the attraction of Cliffy Stone's Hometown Jamboree barn dance in nearby North Hollywood, which pulled in pretty girls from miles around.

Aunt Claudia claimed she could whip all of her brothers

The word soon got out around the base. Before long, Roy had a long list of friends anxious to join him for a weekend at Aunt Claudia's.

At the time of Roy's weekend visits, Claudia Spencer (nee Coats) was in her fifties and living with her sixth husband, Joe Spencer, in Sun Valley.

"She always claimed to have really loved only one man in her life," Roy relates affectionately. "That man was a full-blooded Indian. It took a lot of guts for a white girl to marry an Indian in those days. They were married on Friday in New

Aunt Claudia & Joe Spencer

Mexico and the next morning her ex-boyfriend showed up and gunned her husband down in front of her. 'I don't believe he was even arrested for killing,' she once told me sadly."

Joe Spencer, her sixth husband, wasn't quite as thrilled as Aunt Claudia to see a carload of Marines descend on their small house. It wasn't unusual for him to simply disappear somewhere for the duration of their visit.

"That didn't bother Aunt Claudia one bit," says Roy. "She would often say 'I hope the bastard never comes back!' She really didn't mean it, though, as they stayed together for many years after that."

On Roy's eighteenth birthday he drove to Sun Valley from Camp Pendleton with his two close friends, Curly and Giggles. When they arrived they found Aunt Claudia in high spirits, it being Friday with a whole weekend ahead.

Roy's car had broken down several times on the trip north so Roy asked if he could borrow her car to go to a liquor store. She not only gladly gave him the keys, but five dollars to add to their drinking fund.

"We made the tactical mistake of going into a tavern near the liquor store," Roy remembers. "And somehow, we didn't get back to Aunt Claudia's until Sunday afternoon."

On Sunday morning the time of reckoning was at hand. Roy realized he would have to return Aunt Claudia's car and that she would make the most of their neglectful behavior. On the way to her house, Roy bought a bouquet of flowers and warned his friends to be prepared for an explosive display of temper from Aunt Claudia. Not to worry, though, he said, the bouquet of flowers would handle everything. His friends were a trifle sceptical, but Roy assured them everything would be fine.

True to form, when Aunt Claudia saw them pulling into the driveway she threw a very impressive fit of anger, kicking furniture off the porch. She then made a menacing beeline for the car.

"You little bastard!" she yelled at Roy. "Get the hell out of my goddam son-of-bitchin' car before I kick the hell out of you!"

Roy and his friends were in that delicate state of partial unreality which follows two days and nights of unremitting indulgence. And Aunt Claudia seemed mad enough to carry out the threat and actually drag them all from the car. At the very moment Aunt Claudia leaned toward the open window where Roy sat, Roy whipped out the bouquet of flowers and held them before Aunt Claudia's face.

The transformation was instantaneous. She switched from blazing anger to moony affection — just as Roy said she would.

"Oh, are these for me sweetheart?" she said. Although Roy had predicted what would happen, the sudden transformation was too much for Roy and his friends. They collapsed, doubled over with laughter. Realizing she had been "had," Aunt Claudia switched the anger back on.

"Get your little asses in the house," she yelled, kicking the car fender for good measure. "I'll get lunch ready," she growled and stalked back to the house.

That very special and loving relationship between Roy and his remarkable Aunt Claudia produced a legacy of anecdotes. "Tell us another Aunt Claudia story" became a familiar refrain among his friends in later years. And when Roy does so, the tears of laughter and deep affection flow again, undiminished by time.

Typical of that loving, combative relationship, was a drive by Roy and Aunt Claudia to Texas to visit Aunt Claudia's brother. Roy was approaching the end of his hitch with the Marine Corps and was given a thirty-day leave.

It was the usual hot Southern California summer when they set out, and bound to get much hotter when they climbed out of the Los Angeles basin into desert country. Aunt Claudia suggested to Roy that he buy a window air conditioning unit for the car.

The unit was a "swamp cooler" which works on the principle that air is cooled when it passes over water contained inside. Roy installed the unit on the passenger side window and the next day they set out for Texas.

Within a short time they passed over the mountains and into the shimmering heat of the Mojave Desert. And true enough, the air blowing in through the window and over the cooler was a few degrees cooler. The only snag was that it started to rain drops of water on Aunt Claudia.

Within a short time, Aunt Claudia was soaking wet and looking, as Roy described it, like a "drowned rat." Her blue eyes flashed with indignation as she tried to control her temper. By this time, Roy was struggling equally hard to control his laughter — so much so he was having a hard time keeping the car in a straight line.

"I'm sorry, Aunt Claudia," he managed to blurt out. "I'll fix it when we stop for gas."

"Yeh, you little bastard!" she snapped right back. By now she had half-convinced herself that Roy had rigged the cooler purposely to blow water on her. It was a tailor-made situation for both of them to "get at each other" in their customary fashion. And both took advantage of it.

At the first gas station Roy found a line had worked loose from vibration. He tightened it and announced the problem was solved. Some miles down the road water began to splash on Aunt Claudia again. Roy stopped at the next gas station and stuffed a towel in the window, convincing Aunt Claudia that the problem was now definitely solved.

This solution worked well for a short time, but when the towel was soaking wet it slipped loose and began to flap in Aunt Claudia's face.

The battle with the air cooler lasted all the way to Seymour, Texas. When Roy finally stopped the car outside her brother's house, Aunt Claudia jumped from the car, ripped the cooler from the car window, hurled it to the ground and stomped it into tiny pieces.

"Maybe," said Roy, trying to control his laughter, "we should buy a new one for the trip home."

"Like hell!" she stormed. "Why I'd just as soon burn up as have that damned thing in there wetting me down."

* * * *

As time went on, Roy eased away from gambling. His desire to make something of himself won out over the easy life. Roy set himself up in the used-car business during off-duty hours. He would buy an old junker of a car and fix it up, then "arrange" through one of his friends at base headquarters for a valued base sticker. Without this sticker, a car could not be brought onto the base. Roy's cars were soon in considerable demand.

That business came to a sudden end when one of the Marines who had purchased a car from Roy had an accident.

Roy was holding the papers because the Marine still owed money on the car. "They traced it back and found all these stickers and just closed me up," Roy says.

Undaunted, Roy used the remaining two or three cars to start a car rental business, driving Marines to Tijuana for liberty. Looking back, Roy is convinced he must have led a charmed life to have come through those days unscathed.

"We used to drink what we called shake-em-ups," says Roy. "A mixture of white port and orange juice. We'd just get crazy, no other word for it. I've practically run over highway patrol cops, spun their car around and then give them some story about just leaving for Korea the next day. 'Got a little drunk, officer, and really feel bad about it.' They would say, 'Look, drive slowly until you get back to base.' Today, you'd be buried in jail."

As Roy admits, it is easy enough to look back from today's perspective and see clearly one "should not have done such and such, but back then I was doing whatever seemed to feel best to me at the time."

* * * *

If baseball is our national pastime, then the pitcher is the closest thing in sports to the quintessential American hero: alone on the pitching mound, the focus of all attention. The pitcher needs a special kind of intestinal fortitude to overcome the fear of failure or humiliation. What boy hasn't dreamed of being a major league pitcher — the perfect game, the unbeatable fastball, the perfect inside curve, the fearsome knuckle ball. Most of us find out we don't have the "right stuff" early in life, reconcile to that and go on to other dreams.

As a young boy in Billings, Montana, serving soft drinks to fans at the baseball stadium or playing on the local sand lot, Roy had that dream. He also had an above average measure of the "right stuff." In the Marine Corps he played baseball every chance he got and, with some justification, decided he would try for a career in pro ball when his enlistment was up. He had both the speed and the physique now, standing almost six-foot-three-inches and weighing 190 pounds of hard-packed muscle.

Lying on his bunk at Camp Pendleton one night, Roy felt an excruciating pain in his back and shoulder. It was all he could do not to scream out loud. Eventually the pain began to subside and he rolled over and went to sleep.

"The next morning I woke to find one shoulder blade sticking out like some kind of funny flag at right angles to my back," Roy relates. "I couldn't use my right arm at all. I was plenty scared."

At the base hospital they diagnosed a "minor case" of polio. The polio had been at work for some time and completely wasted the striatus muscle which holds the shoulder blade in place. Roy was in daily therapy for three months but the muscle did not respond.

With typical perseverance and some painful trial and error, Roy found that while he could not pitch hardball, he could still pitch softball. The doctors urged him to continue to play softball to help build up the right side of his back and shoulder.

"So I gave up my dream of being the next Cy Young," Roy says, matter of factly, "but I didn't quit pitching softball until these past few years when business pressures wouldn't allow me to get to the games. I pitched in the Burbank Industrial League for the Sunbank Electronics company team for twenty-one years. One year we went all the way to the All-Country Softball Championship which, I'm proud to say, we won."

No sooner had the dream of a professional baseball career faded when a new and altogether different kind of dream walked into Roy's life. Her name was Patricia Claudette Fish.

Roy had always been quite shy with girls. On weekend visits to Cliffy Stone's Hometown Jamboree, decked out in his Marine uniform, he found himself popular with girls for the first time.

"It was only after I found confidence as a Marine that I had enough nerve to ask a girl for a date," he admits.

Roy began to date one girl regularly. Shortly before his discharge, Roy nerved himself to ask Patricia Fish if she would marry him. Patricia agreed.

The reaction of Aunt Claudia and his Marine friends was not what he expected. They warned him not to jump into marriage so quickly.

"But I thought I knew it all by then," Roy adds ruefully.

On May 26, 1955, Roy was discharged from the Marine Corps. Three days later, he married Patricia Fish.

At 19, Patricia Fish was a very pretty girl with light brown hair and dark blue eyes. Roy admits that at the time he was not looking any further than that — and had little inkling of the responsibilities of marriage, or the adjustment needed in his somewhat reckless lifestyle to make marriage work.

Patricia's mother and father were divorced and her mother had worked hard to provide a home for Patricia and her brother and sister. A decent home, children and a steady husband with a regular job were as close as Patricia came to formulating any goals for herself at that time. Roy admits these were not goals he had given much thought to, if at all.

A lot had happened in the world since Roy entered the Marine Corps. Stalin was dead. Eisenhower was President. The first atomic submarine, Nautilus, was undergoing sea trials. At home, the swooping ducktail haircuts and furrowed Apache came and went, rock and roll dominated the jukeboxes and social observers pointed to the music and the appearance of Beatniks as a sign the society was doomed. That year, 1955, another young man named Sandy Koufax began pitching for the Brooklyn Dodgers.

In California, the fledgling aerospace industry was beginning to stir in response to Russia's bid for missile and outer space supremacy. Although Roy had not the slightest inkling or interest at that time, the aerospace boom in California was to have a profound influence on his life in the decades ahead.

9
A TIME FOR DECISION

The 1950s was a decade of precarious balances. The Eisenhower presidency brought peace and unprecedented material prosperity to middle class Americans and, as the Korean War trudged on to a stalemate, Americans closed up their bomb shelters and dug barbecue pits instead.

At home, Americans watched *Gunsmoke* on television, *The Honeymooners, Ozzie and Harriet*, and *Dinah Shore*. They marvelled as Charles Van Doren knocked off all rivals on the quiz show *Twenty-One* for a record payoff of $129,000.

Among young people, though, there was a growing rebelliousness. Some sociologists point to the fact that this was the first generation to grow up under the threat of nuclear extinction. Others point to a breakdown of social values or the influence of popular domestic gurus like Doctor Benjamin Spock, who advocated permissiveness in regard to child-rearing.

Be that as it may, one thing was clear by the mid-1950s — a rebellion of some kind was underway. The Beat Generation emerged — many of them disillusioned Korean War veterans. They were a small foretaste of the Hippies to come in the next generation. The language changed in streets and high schools. Now everything was cool, real gone, the most, way out, smooth, real George, flip and hip. By 1955, teenage violence was reaching alarming proportions. Gang warfare and crime were rising faster than the statisticians could count.

There were other undercurrents smoldering. In Montgomery, Alabama, a scholarly young preacher was about to get involved in a bus boycott by blacks. His name was Martin Luther King, Jr.

It was in the middle of this decade that Roy Coats was discharged from the Marine Corps on May 26, 1955. He had two hundred dollars mustering out pay, most of which he

Roy & Pat at wedding

promptly gave to his fiance, Patricia Fish, to settle a traffic accident she had been involved in the week before.

At nineteen, the only rebellion Roy Coats was interested in was a rebellion against poverty and failure. And for that he didn't need the approval of his peers or to run with a gang. He was going to get married, then put all his efforts into making something of himself. Unlike so many of his contemporaries, Roy was not searching for values. He had long since found them.

As though in compensation for the years he spent without a mother, three women turned up at Roy's wedding. Each claimed to be his rightful mother. One was Sephronie, his real mother. The other was Margaret Baum, whose claim rested mostly on spiritual grounds. The third was the widow of Roy's natural father, Eugene Coats. This was not only a surprise to Roy, but everyone else. No one could figure out how she even heard of the wedding.

With only twenty-five dollars in his pocket, Roy's honeymoon plans looked pretty bleak until Ernest Baum came to the rescue with two hundred dollars. With that, Roy and his new bride set off on a motoring honeymoon in Roy's old car.

This mobile honeymoon would fulfill several desires — one was to show Patricia some of the country that had so impressed Roy as a young boy on his journey to California. Another was to visit Eakle Colliflower, his mother's former husband, who now owned a small service station in Phoenix.

Some time earlier, Eakle had suggested to Roy that when he finished his time in the Marines he might like to go into business with him. Just the ring of it sounded good to Roy — going into business. He wanted something he could really devote all his energies to and build a worthwhile career. Something that would be his own creation.

As soon as Roy saw the service station he knew in his heart it wasn't what he had in mind, but Eakle was so happy to see Roy and painted such a glowing picture of the possibilities that Roy put aside his misgivings. He would give it a try, and return to Phoenix when the honeymoon was over.

To speed them along safely, Eakle loaned Roy his new car. They took off for Colorado along the Million Dollar Highway to Silverton and those same mountains where Roy had been stranded one cold mountain winter.

Roy pointed out the ranches he had worked on and showed Patricia the town of Ouray, where he had been stranded by the snowstorm. He even showed her the house where he had been forced to shelter, but thoughtfully neglected to mention the girl who had shared his evenings by the glowing wood stove.

From the Colorado mountains they drove south, through the famous mining town of Silverton, then on to beautiful Durango, with its lumber mills and cattle ranches. Crossing into New Mexico, Roy told Patricia about his experiences as a roughneck in Farmington. They drove through the town of Shiprock and finally to Gallup, to pick up Highway 66 on its swing through Arizona to the West Coast.

It was while driving through Gallup that Roy had the first intimation that marriage might involve more than he had originally envisioned. Driving through a run-down section of the city, they passed an old Indian who was falling down drunk.

"Pat couldn't believe that people could get themselves into such a condition," Roy recalls. "I thought to myself at the time that I'd seen dozens of drunks worse than this one on skid row in Oklahoma City as a boy. It didn't seem to me this one drunk was even worth remarking upon."

But Patricia couldn't get over it and kept expressing her surprise and disgust. For the first time, Roy realized just how different their backgrounds and temperaments were and how little she knew of his past struggles and the consequent depth of his ambition and drive to be a success.

"I began to think then how I'd taken on the responsibility for the care of someone who had led such a sheltered childhood," Roy adds, "and what it might take to keep her happy."

In Phoenix, Roy rented a small apartment for one month, and went to work with Eakle. But time had brought many changes to both Roy and Eakle Colliflower. Although they got along together very well, Eakle still dwelt in a slow-moving world of his own. He much preferred to sit down with similarly unambitious friends outside the service station than invest the time needed to rescue the small business from its obvious decline.

Within a few days it was clear to Roy that Eakle was not about to change his ways. He told Eakle that he appreciated the opportunity but felt there really wasn't sufficient work to justify two people in the business.

"Well, Roy, I can see what you mean," Eakle said, good-naturedly. "No hard feelings, son, and the best of luck to you out there in California," Roy remembers him saying.

California 1955. Transition time, with "Rock Around the Clock" by Bill Haley and the Comets reverberating from jukeboxes and car radios as the top-selling record. It seemed strange company for the other best selling records that year, like Mitch Miller's orchestra and chorus singing "Yellow Rose of Texas" and Perez Prado's "Cherry Pink and Apple Blossom White."

Scanning the Help Wanted columns, Roy came across an announcement that General Telephone was hiring. With his recent Marine Corps training in telephone systems and cables,

Roy felt he was a likely candidate. General Telephone thought otherwise.

Because of his court martial and time in the brig, Roy was not given the usual Honorable Discharge, but a General Discharge Under Honorable Conditions. The personnel interviewer at General Telephone had no idea how much self-control Roy exerted on himself when the interviewer looked down his nose at Roy's application because of his discharge.

Roy's next stop was the personnel office of Lockheed Corporation in Burbank. Roy was hired to work on the swing-shift in the plating department. It was dull and uninspiring work, but it paid the rent and put food on the table. Working nights enabled Roy to "keep a sharp eye out for opportunities," as Ernest Baum used to tell him.

With the economy booming, there was a demand for scrap metal. During his spare time, Roy cut up junk cars and hauled the scrap to a dealer in Los Angeles. With this extra income he began to put a little money aside for the future.

Then Roy noticed an old car in the Lockheed parking lot. It had been modified by cutting out the sides and installing shelves to make a mobile display counter. Roy found the owner, bought the car on time payments and went into the fresh fruit and vegetable business during his daytime off-shift hours.

When his swing-shift ended at about one-thirty in the morning, Roy drove to the produce market in Los Angeles for fresh fruit and vegetables. He returned home to sleep until seven or eight in the morning. After a quick breakfast, he drove to a corner on Glenoaks Boulevard in Sun Valley and put up his sign.

Occasionally he borrowed a friend's truck and drove to the San Joaquin Valley for a load of potatoes. These were broken down into small sacks for resale. Within a few weeks he had made enough profit from his fruit and vegetables to fully pay for the car.

Business went along well for some months. Then Lockheed decided to transfer Roy to the day-shift and a different job. This meant he would have to give up his thriving fruit and vegetable business, and the thought of it made Roy quite unhappy. His dissatisfaction was readily apparent to his shift foreman, who mentioned to Roy he didn't look happy.

"You are sure right about that," Roy agreed. At the end

of that shift he quit his job with Lockheed.

Roy redoubled his efforts with the roadside stand, but the payback did not equal his efforts. There was no way he could get the business to support them. Patricia was not working and was now pregnant. Within a few weeks he sold the car for a good profit and went to work for his wife's grandfather in the roofing business.

Roofing is not an easy occupation. Even today, with hydraulic lifts to carry the ninety pound packs of roofing shingles and pumps to get the hot tar to the roof, workers earn their money the hard way. When Roy went to work, everything had to be carried up ladders by hand. As a newcomer, his job, of course, was to carry it up.

He was employed as a helper, which meant tending the hot fuming tar kettle and carrying the tar up to the roof in five gallon buckets. Although he was still in excellent physical condition from his three years in the Marine Corps, the work was brutally demanding.

There was also the added pressure from the knowledge that there were always men eager to replace anyone who lagged on the job. The reason was simply that the base pay was higher than most other unskilled or semi-skilled work.

Roy admits that in his first week he almost keeled over more than once during hot summer days in the San Fernando and San Gabriel Valleys around Los Angeles. With ambient temperatures hovering around one hundred degrees, the absorbent qualities of the black tar, combined with the reflection from the mica crystals in the roofing materials, boosted the temperature to one-hundred-and-twenty on the roof.

Roy stuck with it and eventually began to enjoy the job. As happened in the Marine Corps, Roy found the challenge of competing against older and more experienced men to be exhilarating. He particularly enjoyed the sense of accomplishment at the end of each day when he could see what his efforts had produced. Within a few months, he was promoted to roofer's assistant and then to crew lead man.

Roofing is a seasonal business. With the rainy winter season in California, Roy knew he would soon be out of a job. He was also going to be a father before long, so once again he turned to the classified columns to find more permanent work.

An opening for an expediter at Pacific Mercury Television

caught his attention. At that time, Pacific Mercury made Silvertone television sets for Sears and cabling assemblies for Boeing Aircraft. Roy had not the slightest idea what an expediter was, but reasoned that if they could tell him what the job was exactly, then he could do it.

His confidence and determination got him the job. He was assigned to expedite materials in the cable assembly section that worked on electrical wiring assemblies for Boeing Aircraft. Roy's job was to communicate with purchasing, the stockroom and the wire cut and code department to make sure all the parts needed for each day's production were on hand for the cable assemblers.

These cable assemblies, or wiring harnesses, are quite complex. They consist of precise bundles of wires needed to relay the pilot's control operations to the engines, flaps, landing gear and other equipment. The cable assemblies also carry all the information from sensor points throughout the aircraft to the cockpit instruments.

This was Roy's introduction to a manufacturing process and he found it fascinating. He had to coordinate with purchasing and establish priorities and targets so that wiring and connectors were ordered and received to meet assembly production schedules. These schedules had to mesh exactly with the production schedule of the Boeing factory, so that the assembled cables were on hand for final installation in the aircraft.

Roy was too busy to notice, but events were shaping in the outside world that would have a direct and lasting effect on his future. He was too busy because, in addition to his full-time job, Roy worked from five to midnight at a local liquor store, and the weekends he spent cutting up junk cars for scrap metal.

In November, 1956, Soviet Premier Nikita Khrushchev boasted "We will bury you!," referring to Russia's development of intercontinental missiles that could deliver atomic warheads almost anywhere on earth.

The following year, Russia would be first in space with Sputnik One. A race was underway between Russia and America in the aerospace and missile field and the most powerful nation in the world was going to have to play catch-up with the Russians.

With his job in cable assembly, Roy Coats was sitting

right in the middle of the action. Within months, one of the most phenomenal industry growths in history was about to take place — much of it centered in California.

In 1956 Roy received a telephone call from an ex-employee of Pacific Mercury. The call was an offer for Roy to join him in a new cable assembly company being formed at Glendale Airport. It was a better job and at considerably higher pay. Roy jumped at the offer. The company was Pacific Automation Products, Inc. and Roy was one of the early employees.

The company had been formed to build cable assemblies for the new Atlas missile project. Within eighteen months, Pacific Automation would grow to over eleven hundred employees!

Unofficially, the missile race had been on for some time, but when Russia propelled the first artificial satellite (Sputnik One) into space on October 4, 1957, it not only caught the attention of the world, it galvanized the Administration and Congress to pour massive funds into aerospace development.

Almost overnight, the stocks of publicly owned corporations like Boeing, Lockheed, McDonnell-Douglas, General Dynamics, Northrup, Chance-Vought, Convair and the rest rocketed to giddy heights. Hundreds of new companies set up shop to become suppliers to the main aerospace contractors around the nation, who were recipients of Defense Department contracts.

The assembly and test areas for rockets was a veritable Sargasso Sea of electrical cables and complex electronics. Frequently, the outlets and connector hook-ups between cable systems and between various sections of the rockets differed among the major contractors.

Pacific Automation specialized in all types of electrical cable assemblies for aerospace clients. The rapid growth and complexity of the system, and the need for custom-designed connector accessories was forcing the company into a secondary area of business — the design and fabrication of accessories to join together the jungle of different cable assemblies.

"It was the wildest damned place I'd ever seen," says Roy, "but I loved every minute of it."

Enthusiastic confusion was the order of the day. At one end of a large aircraft hanger, Pacific Automation employees were in a desperate race to supply the Atlas missile programs with ever increasingly complex cables, which were always needed, "yesterday." At the other end of the hanger, Grand Central Aircraft was testing aircraft engines.

"The noise was unbelieveable," Roy recalls. "People had to scream into the telephone to make themselves heard. Even so, employees regularly worked from six in the morning until nine or ten at night, six and even seven days a week, because morale was sky-high."

Roy became curious as to why morale remained high. The working conditions were poor to dreadful. The hours of work were extremely long and the pace was frantic. The answers he came up with would become part of his own success formula in later years.

"As far as the company was concerned," Roy explains, "if an employee knew what he was doing and *cared* about what he was doing, he or she could do no wrong. Also, they paid generously for the overtime work. And, most important, there was no time for boredom to develop or for petty griping because everyone was so busy they didn't have time for anything but the job in hand."

The bottom line, as Roy sees it, is that "busy people are happy people." When the work slacks off and people start standing around, time drags and you're going to have morale problems every time.

"If you only have enough work for two-and-a-half people," says Roy, "then make sure you've only got two people working on it. Don't hire that third person until you've got enough work for more than three people."

With morale so high, a real team spirit developed at Pacific Automation. The employees worked hard and played hard together after work. Although, Roy admits with a grin, most of that "play" took place in a neighborhood tavern.

"But we all showed up at six the next morning," he adds. "Without fail."

At Pacific Mercury and now at Pacific Automation, Roy found himself with a very hard-working, but very fast-living crowd of young people. At Pacific Mercury, there were about one thousand women on the payroll. At Pacific Automation, it wasn't too long before the company had expanded to the point where there were about six hundred women on the payroll.

"Here I was," says Roy, "a young marine, a year out of the service...it's hard to stay out of trouble, it really is. And

I didn't work very hard at staying out of trouble either. There were more crossed up relationships at Pacific Automation, more marriages and divorces...it was just a very turbulent time. Sometimes I look back," Roy admits, "and wonder how I survived all that craziness. I had a license to be arrested at all times."

Roy's experience with electrical connectors in his previous job as expediter proved to be a needed asset. He soon became the resident connector expert at Pacific Automation.

Within a short time, the company created a new department exclusively to handle the mushrooming demand for specialized connectors.

It was Roy's responsibility to ensure that electrical connectors were ordered and received as needed by the production department. He was also responsible for any modification or repairs needed. It wasn't long before the company had a full blown connector repair section, with several people working in it full-time.

The electrical connectors on the market at that time were only designed to fit a relatively small number of standard cable assemblies. In the booming missile and aerospace program, non-standard applications were becoming the rule as engineers fished and fumbled their way through development of this new technology.

Although he didn't know it then, Roy was not only in on the ground floor of what was to become a fifty million dollars a year electrical connector accessories industry — he *was* the ground floor.

Twenty-six days after Sputnik One began beeping man's first extra-terrestial message from space, Roy Coats turned twenty-two. Already the manager of a department, he was about to become general manager of a whole new division.

Roy proposed to management that they set up the equipment to manufacture connector accessories. In his proposal, he pointed out that problems in the area were continuing to grow and he needed more space to organize the work. He also pointed out that if Pacific Automation was running into these problems with connectors, then the manufacturers of cable assemblies and aerospace equipment around the country were having the same problems. There was, he said, an opportunity for Pacific Automation to become a supplier of connector accessories to these companies, in addition to taking care of its own needs.

The way to exploit this opportunity, he said, was to set up a separate division or subsidiary company under a different name. That way, companies directly competitive to Pacific Automation would not be put in the position of buying connectors from a direct competitor.

Management recognized a good idea when they saw it. Within days they had formed Glenair Incorporated in a small building across the street. Roy was appointed general manager with only one employee to help him — a young girl to handle the paperwork.

While no one expressed any qualms to Roy about appointing a twenty-two-year-old as general manager, neither did management expect anything more than a modest return.

Roy was now a one-man band again. He ram-rodded production, inspected all components, then labeled, packed and shipped them to the growing list of companies that were — as Roy predicted — happy to find a supplier of non-standard connector accessories. He also handled all the sales and promotion himself, in addition to supplying Pacific's needs.

As Roy describes it, his job was to make the accessories "fit." If they didn't fit exactly right, they were not acceptable. Precision was the order of the day. As a pioneer in custom accessories, there were no comprehensive catalog of parts and specifications such as you find today. Roy obtained samples of connector applications from other companies and trained himself to keep a running inventory of specifications in his head.

Within a relatively short time, Roy became extremely proficient at making short-cuts to mate a part from one connector design to a new application in a new design. It was this proficiency that enabled him to meet the impossibly short deadlines of aerospace companies, who were themselves scrambling to keep tight production schedules. The word began to circulate that if you had a connector problem, call Roy Coats at Glenair.

Meanwhile, the owners of Pacific and Glenair left Roy to his own devices. When Roy needed anything, he went to see Marv Borden, one of the partners who had befriended him. Naturally, management hoped the operation would show a small profit. They were stunned when, after only six months of operations, Roy grossed one hundred thousand dollars in sales with a profit of sixty thousand dollars.

Roy was still a novice as far as the financial workings of business were concerned. He had no appreciation at the time what an exceptional performance that was. The owners of Pacific Automation, however, did.

Almost overnight, Pacific Automation management was swarming all over Glenair. Unfortunately, although they recognized a profitable operation when they saw it, they did not know enough to leave a successful operation alone and simply give Roy the support and backup he needed. Conflicting orders from half a dozen management executives at Pacific began to flow daily into Roy's little subsidiary. From a benign disinterest, management was now telling him not only what to do, but how to do it.

This experience taught Roy an invaluable lesson. As a result, he made it a rule that every manager or department head working for him first learns every single function in that department before he was allowed to give orders. And that means doing each job within the department, not just watching others.

"Until that time," says Roy, "he is not really capable of making the best possible decision."

At about this time, Roy became aware of the true ownership situation at Glenair Inc. — the stock was owned by six equal partners. He had no quarrel with this, per se, but problems were developing from the fact that he was receiving orders from several management people at the same time. One, in particular, was an ex-Air Force officer who gave orders as if he was still in the military, and really rubbed Roy the wrong way. As a result, thoughts of going into business for himself began surfacing.

A short time later, Roy's time of decision arrived. He remembered Ernest Baum's advice to always be on the lookout for an opportunity and to grasp it when it came. Roy felt that opportunity might now be within his grasp.

"I had no real idea of what it took to run a business — of receivables and payables, balance sheets, marketing, taxes and the hundred and one details of routine business management," Roy admits. "But I did have a willingness to try."

It was that "willingness to try" that got Roy across that invisible but formidable line which separates dreaming about doing something and actually going out and doing it.

"That was the hardest decision of all to make," Roy says. "I'd worked hard for eight thousand dollars, but I was willing to risk losing all of it. I accepted the fact that I might fail, but if I did, I was young enough to do it all over again. And again and again if needed."

Roy was about to go out and play some real hard ball.

10
FROM DREAM TO REALITY

High in the Top Ten record charts that summer of 1958 was the song "All I Have to Do is Dream," by the Everly Brothers. Roy Coats was about to go one step further and turn his dream into reality.

It was a momentous summer other ways as well. President Eisenhower set a fateful precedent by sending U.S. Marines to Lebanon. The National Aeronautics and Space Administration was spun off as a separate entity from the Department of Defense. As N.A.S.A. it would soon become a household word.

Across America, suburbia was now in full flower, along with commuting, lawnmowing and rising taxes to support all those schools and shopping centers. These were "baby boom" years. Between 1950 and 1960, children in the age group of five to fourteen went from 24.3 million to 35.5 million. Bicycle production shot up from 2 to 3.8 million, encyclopedia sales went from 72 million to 300 million dollars and sales of musical instruments went from 86 to 149 million dollars.

Testifying to the popularity of the cocktail circuit in suburbia, gin production went from 6 to 19 million gallons, vodka from 0.1 to 9 million gallons. Yes, and aspirin sales went from 12 to 18 million pounds.

California was growing at a staggering pace as spreading suburbs gobbled up orange groves and valleys once dotted with ranches and farms. The aerospace industry in California lured engineers and skilled workers from all over the nation.

In 1956, Jackie Gleason said of Elvis Presley, "He can't last. I tell you flatly — he can't last." And that's what the owner of Pacific Automation and Glenair thought when Roy handed in his resignation and left to form his own company. Like Jackie Gleason, they were woefully wrong.

If Roy Coats had known more about running a business perhaps he might have sought advice from a lawyer or accountant. And since, by their nature, lawyers and accountants tend to be conservative, they might have dissuaded him. They could have pointed out that for one so young he was already general manager with a fine career ahead of him. But Roy didn't know any lawyers or accountants then. What he had in abundance, though, was determination and the willingness to work hard. That is a combination that has brought more success than a legion of lawyers and accountants.

When Roy resigned, he offered to take whatever time was necessary to fully train a replacement. In doing so, he ensured that Glenair would successfully continue in the connector accessory business.

It is ironic that Glenair would not only become Roy Coats major competitor in the connector accessories field — even to this day — but would also outlive its parent company, Pacific Automation, which sank into bankruptcy during the Sixties.

Another irony was that the man chosen to replace Roy as general manager of Glenair, and to be trained by him, was Corky Kirk. After nearly twenty years with Glenair, Corky Kirk ended up working for Roy Coats as sales manager at Sunbank Electronics.

Reflecting on that beginning today, Roy had only one regret. He felt that he needed time to prepare a plan for his new company so did not tell Pacific Automation he was leaving to start a competitive company. Instead, he chose to tell his employer he was rejoining Ernest Baum in a new enterprise.

The decision to not tell his employers the truth was one that "I've had cause not to feel good about over the years," admits Roy, "but I cannot honestly say if the exact same conditions existed I wouldn't do it again."

Roy knew that going up against such a power in the industry as Pacific Automation was going to be tough enough, without giving them the opportunity to sink his boat before it got launched. "I was so convinced at the time that they had this kind of power, I felt if I told them the truth I would never be able to get through the door to see a potential customer. Over the years, though, I've learned that they probably couldn't have stopped me, but at the time it seemed to be too much of a jeopardy."

It is a testimony to Roy's innate honesty that this should

still concern him more than 25 years later. In truth, it was an action that many businessmen would say was only prudent and is done every day. But Roy felt he had let down his friend, Marv Borden, by not telling him the truth at the time. "He had been a good friend to me," says Roy, "even though he was my boss. He was more than that, though — I trusted him and he trusted me; I liked him and I didn't feel good about it, even though today we're good friends."

On the face of it , the odds were stacked against him. He had only eight thousand dollars and no bank would give him credit. His biggest asset was that he knew the connector business inside and out. He knew who bought what and how much. He knew what it took to make the parts and make them well. As Andrew Jackson once said: "One man with courage makes a majority."

The connector accessories business is predominantly a custom-order business, even today. Attempts have been made at standardization, but there is still a bewildering multitude of different size shells, clamps, threads and seals. Today, Sunbank Electronics maintains a file of over one-and-a-half million different drawings of accessories developed for customers around the world.

Simply put, cylindrical connectors are similar in principle to the small cylindrical connectors which join a television cable to the back of the television set. In the aerospace industry they are used to mate two different cables or bundles of control wires. Such cables can consist of hundreds of individual wires and require much more complex connectors with extremely precise threads, bores and counterbores to exactly mate the different cables.

Fortunately for Roy, there were only a few cylindrical connector styles to deal with in 1958. His priority task, though, was to design a marketing brochure illustrating his products and get that out to his potential customers.

Roy rented a small building on Burbank Boulevard, not far from the massive Lockheed Corporation complex near the Burbank Airport. He bought a desk, had the utilities and telephone connected, bought a typewriter and some stationery and hired a typist.

Roy burned the midnight oil over the brochure, but finally it came together. He spent long days on the telephone compiling a list of engineers and others who made buying decisions in the industry. Within a week he had his mailing list and sent out several hundred brochures. Orders began to trickle in. The eight thousand dollars was going fast on rent, salary for the typist, office supplies, tables for inspection and packing the connectors, and telephone calls. A drafting table and drafting machine to draw up specifications for the machine shop ate up more of his thinning capital.

At that time a typical connector accessory cost about eight dollars and most orders were for small quantities of twenty-five to fifty pieces. Even though the accessories were highly specialized items, the market would not bear more than a twenty percent profit level. It took a great deal of work to make forty dollars profit on a two hundred dollar order.

Without capital, Roy knew he had to persuade his various suppliers and machine shops to give him credit. In other words, they would get paid when he got paid. He didn't try to flim-flam, but laid out his position for them in typically honest fashion. The suppliers trusted him. Some had been there themselves. They would wait for their money.

His next step was to reinforce and extend the personal contacts he had already made in the aerospace industry. In other words, get out and sell what he had to offer.

It was obvious that selling ability would have a lot to do with whether Sunbank would survive or not. Roy drew heavily on his past learning experiences with Ernest Baum, Jim Kaufman and other salesman he had seen at work.

"When everything else is going wrong," Roy says, "that's when you really need a good salesman. I didn't shy away from selling when the opportunity arose. Besides, I couldn't afford to hire a salesman."

Roy's attitude towards selling and his basic integrity played a vital role in ensuring the survival of Sunbank. The secret, he discovered, was not to be found in subterfuge, in finely tuned sales programs or in playing the smart huckster. What it required was a single-minded devotion to honesty.

"This dictated the manner of my approach to customers," Roy relates. "It was sincere and straightforward. It is then just a matter of convincing a customer he should be involved with you. After a period of time your honesty and sincerity comes through.

"Customers sold on that basis will be customers that make your success in the future," Roy adds, "because from this you will get recommendations and word-of-mouth advertising that you never dreamed was possible."

While it takes guts to hang a shingle over the door and announce to the world you are in business, it is another thing altogether to get the cash flowing in to survive. The real challenge in business is to survive and prosper. Persistence is the name of the game.

Well, persist Roy did, working eighteen hours a day, seven days a week. He looked after the billing, invoicing and promotion mailings. He made drawings for the machine shops. He personally checked each accessory against the drawings for quality. Then he packed and shipped them to customers. On top of that, he was the only one to answer technical inquiries from customers and make the sales calls.

Despite this grueling schedule there was a sense of satisfaction that he was actually doing it — he was running his own business and it would be solely on his efforts that it would survive or fail. There is a joy in that, says Roy, that is hard to describe.

The first six months were literally a hand-to-mouth existence. Roy paid himself just enough to cover food for his family and his GI mortgage loan, which came to just over one hundred dollars a month. When a check came in from a customer, he would pay his vital suppliers first — the machine shop, foundry and plating company that made his connector accessories. What was left went to pay fixed overheads such as telephone, office supplies, utilities and his single typist.

"There wasn't a lot of financial planning involved," Roy admits with a smile. "It was just a matter of survival."

In addition to his growing reputation as the man to call if you needed answers in a hurry, there was another factor on his side — the time element. In the aerospace industry, time is of the essence. Connector accessories have to be there when the customer demands them. A few days or even a few hours delay can slow down and halt an entire project worth many millions of dollars. At Glenair and then with his own company, Roy went to extraordinary lengths to ensure accessories were delivered on time.

For example, when talking to engineers, Roy would find out that a new project was about to go into the engineering stage and would need fast delivery. Roy would go ahead and make the connectors, without the benefit of an order. "When it came time to place an order, I'd have them ready and be able to give them super quick delivery," says Roy. "They couldn't believe it. Someone else would quote them two weeks and I'd quote them two days. At the same time," Roy adds, "it got that money in fast for me. And I needed it."

Roy knew full well that reliability was the key to his success. So did his competitors. Rumors began to circulate in the industry that Roy was going bankrupt or that he could not deliver his products on time. Roy had to scotch these quickly or his fledgling company would never get off the ground.

His handling was typically forthright. He walked into each customer's office and said that not only would he deliver the product on time at a fair price, but would personally guarantee both delivery and quality.

Aware of Roy's track record, a number of customers were not put off by the rumors, but it was a touch-and-go situation. When Roy proved as good as his word, the rumors fell on deaf ears and finally ceased. Now his growing reputation for on-time deliveries had the phone at Sunbank ringing off the hook and he had to add additional lines. But phone calls alone don't put money in the cash register.

The immature nature of the accessories business was such that a supplier, like Roy, might spend many hours or days talking with engineers over a period of many weeks. It could be as long as a year down the line before any major orders for accessories resulted.

"We would get called in at the design stage of a project," Roy relates. "They would order a small quantity of accessories for the mock-up project. But not until months later, when the production got underway, would the major orders for accessories be received."

An example of this occurred on one of the first sales calls Roy made. Roy spent several hours with an engineer at the Jet Propulsion Laboratory in Pasadena.

"I was showing him how to pick and match accessory part numbers," Roy recalls. "I felt sure I was wasting my time because the engineer didn't seem to know very much about connector accessories. I wrote off JPL as a customer. Seven months later the phone rang. The engineer had picked Sunbank to provide the accessories for the Sergeant Missile

Project — a substantial and profitable project."

It was a vivid lesson in the value of research and good public relations.

Other and less obvious factors were working in Roy's favor at that time — the payoff from his earlier attention to quality and service while at Pacific Automation. As the decade of the 1950s drew to a close, the aerospace industry was at the height of its incredible growth and flux. New companies were springing up, others were merging and some couldn't meet the demands and simply folded. Engineers were at a premium and talent scouts were busy at the major companies trying to attract engineers from other companies. It was a situation not unlike that existing in today's microprocessor-computer field.

Engineers Roy had known and worked with at Pacific Automation were now showing up on the engineering teams of aerospace companies all around the country. When the time came to specify connector accessories, many thought of Roy.

"And when I made that first delivery on time I had a repeat customer," says Roy. "People really appreciate getting things when you tell them they're going to get them."

It was just such a call from one of the accounts Roy had serviced during his time at Glenair that finally gave Roy his first bit of "breathing room."

The account was Chrysler Corporation in Detroit, then at work on one of the missile development programs. Knowing Chrysler was already an established account with Glenair — his chief competitor — Roy decided to pull out all the stops and fly to Detroit. The fare was a big investment for Roy at that time, but he knew he had to take a chance in the hope of securing a large order.

Roy couldn't afford to waste any time in leisurely preparation for the flight, he worked frantically at filling orders almost until departure time of the flight. He just had time to throw some brochures and drawings into his small bag before driving to the airport.

When the plane landed at the old Willow Run Airport near Detroit, Roy stepped out of the plane and experienced a severe reality adjustment. In the haste and concentration on business, he had overlooked the fact that while his thin suit was just fine for a California winter, January in Detroit was something else altogether.

"It was like stepping into a deep freeze," Roy recalls. "I was shaking with cold by the time I got to the motel near the Chrysler missile plant in Warren. Even with extra blankets I couldn't get warm enough to sleep properly."

The next morning, Roy tried to defrost his body with numerous cups of coffee, but by the time he reached the Chrysler plant he was again shaking like a leaf.

Roy's contact at the Chrysler plant was a man named Andy Anderson, who later became a close friend and colleague. Andy took one look at Roy's trembling body, clad in a thin California suit, and erupted in a belly laugh. Many years later, Roy would arrange to have his own belly laugh at Andy's expense.

Andy Anderson hustled Roy inside and the Chrysler engineers he had come to meet also found the situation enormously amusing. If nothing else it did "break the ice" between them and soon Roy was in deep discussion with the engineers over the most effective use of connector accessories.

At lunch following the discussion, it took several stiff drinks to control Roy's shivering. As they left the restaurant, one of the engineers loaned Roy his topcoat for the trip home to California.

What really warmed Roy, though, was the order Chrysler gave him for sixteen thousand dollars worth of accessories. It was the start of an uptrend for Sunbank Electronics. Roy had crossed his own personal Rubicon and could now begin to think about expanding his woefully understaffed company.

11
A COSTLY MISTAKE

That last year of the decade there was a sense of well-being in the nation. We had lived through ten years of high tension in the Cold War. Korea was now a distant memory, although the Chinese invasion of Tibet and the flight of the Dalai Lama in March, 1959, sent shock-waves around the world.

In Cuba, Batista and his henchmen had fled the country leaving it in charge of a bearded revolutionary called Castro. In Washington, the prevailing feeling was that Castro was a man they could reasonably deal with.

At home, the St. Lawrence Seaway opened in April, allowing ocean ships to travel deep into the Midwest to pick up grain and iron ore. Eisenhower, looking ahead to the end of his second term as President, bestowed his blessings on Richard Nixon for the upcoming 1960 Primaries. Crew-cuts and flat-tops were the hair style of the day and the new Los Angeles Dodgers won their first World Series, four games to two over Chicago.

Among the top ten records that year was "Mack the Knife" by Bobby Darin, and "The Battle of New Orleans" by Johnny Horten. The book everyone was talking about was *Exodus*, by Leon Uris.

Roy Coats was about to experience his own exodus before the year was out, but that was the last thing on his mind as he contemplated the growing pile of orders from Chrysler and other major defense contractors.

His success had brought a new headache. He had overextended himself. To fill the new orders he needed more production — more space, more employees and more equipment. He was facing the crunch known as under-capitalization. It alone has sent more companies onto the rocks than almost any other cause.

Roy believed the best solution to his problem was to make the connector accessories himself, instead of having them made by a subcontractor outside. That would give him tighter quality control, higher production, and improve his ability to meet tight deadlines.

The lathes, drill presses and other equipment he would need would cost him about one hundred thousand dollars. With his order books and proposal for expansion, Roy went around to various banks shopping for a loan. The bankers agreed that what Sunbank urgently needed was capital to expand but, sorry, they were not about to provide it.

This left Roy with one alternative, as he saw it then — take on a partner who had either the capital or the equipment he needed.

The most likely candidate for partnership was the owner of a machine shop already producing accessories for Roy. In a short time, Sunbank had become its biggest source of revenue. Roy reasoned he was a good machinist and their dealings so far had been quite friendly.

Roy made a simple but attractive offer; half of Sunbank for half of his machine shop. In other words, a fifty-fifty partnership. Because of limited business experience and unsuspicious nature, Roy did not think to insist on maintaining operational control of Sunbank.

The owner was smart enough to know a good deal when he saw one. He would no longer have to worry that another machine shop would make Roy a better deal and take away the business. On top of that he would also share in the profits from Roy's considerable energy and expertise in the connector accessories business.

"Knowing what I know today, I probably could have survived without the partnership," Roy admits, "but I didn't know it then. Uppermost in my mind was the need to respond to customer's orders on a timely basis. At that time, I just didn't think I could get Sunbank to fly unless I had control of my own manufacturing operation."

Human frailties and differences being what they are, business partnerships can often be just as difficult to maintain as any marriage. And when partnerships dissolve can be just as messy as any divorce. That was a lesson Roy had yet to learn, but once learned it was a lesson he never forgot.

Implicit in the concept of equal working partners is the

fact that both partners will work equally hard. Unfortunately, as George Orwell pointed out in his novel, *Animal Farm*, some feel they are more equal than others.

Roy was working himself "silly," seven days a week, selling accessories faster than they were being made. Roy's partner confined his activities to production of accessories. This left Roy with all the front office work — managing the business, quality control, expediting parts, shipping, promotion and sales. It was soon obvious to Roy he would have to hire additional help to enable him to continue with the all-important sales trips. Without them the flow of business would wither away.

One of Roy's most crucial trips during that time was to the massive Martin Aircraft headquarters complex in Baltimore. Roy had been introduced to one of the Martin engineers while visiting Chrysler in Detroit. He now received an invitation to visit Martin to show what Sunbank could do for them.

Roy desperately wanted a crack at the Martin business, but uppermost in his mind was the expense of flying to Baltimore and back. He called the engineer on the telephone and explained that Sunbank was only a small company. It would be hard for him to justify such a trip, he said, without a reasonable certainty that he could receive a big enough order to cover his outlay.

The engineer was insistent. "Roy, I'm telling you, it will definitely be worth your while to come out here and talk to our crew," he said.

At 8:30 on a Monday morning, Roy stood in front of the Martin headquarters, his briefcase stuffed with brochures, drawings and sample accessories. The engineer met Roy in the imposing lobby and led him through a maze of corridors and offices until they finally arrived at a large conference room.

"I felt as though the floor dropped right away from under my feet," Roy recalls.

Seated around a large table were twenty Martin engineers, all looking at Roy, waiting to see what the "hot-shot connector specialist" from California had to say.

"My mouth dried up so badly it felt as if I had a mouthful of chalk," Roy remembers. "All I could think of was that here I was — a twenty-three-year-old punk kid — supposed to show something to these engineers and top management for one of the biggest aircraft companies in the East. It was a bit tense, to say the least."

Roy managed to fish and fumble his way through the first few minutes of his presentation, explaining the various accessories Sunbank could provide. Thankfully, this was quickly followed by a brisk question and answer session on accessories. Roy began to relax. Here he was on solid ground. He knew his business and could handle every question like an expert.

"An engineer would say he had a 13 triple 7 cable and wanted to hook it up with a strain relief and moisture seal and what did we have available?" Roy explains, "I would pull out my brochure or a drawing and show them all the options available. All of a sudden I was getting their close attention."

The session went on for several hours. Then each department head came into the conference room separately and Roy went over the whole subject again, spelling out the part numbers for them.

Elated, Roy returned to California, convinced orders would surely follow soon. A month went by, then another and still no order from the Martin Aircraft Company. Roy finally called the engineer who had invited him to Baltimore. The engineer apologized for the delay. He explained their program was a large one and it took time to get everything in motion.

"By this time I was convinced that after all my groundwork they had probably subcontracted the work to a local parts manufacturer," says Roy. "The only satisfaction I had was that I knew that if they did subcontract to a newcomer to the business, he did not understand the real secret of tolerances in accessories."

But the engineer from Martin was as good as his word. Within a few weeks, Sunbank received an order for thirty-five thousand dollars worth of accessories. Over the next four-and-one-half years, Sunbank averaged forty thousand dollars worth of accessories each month with the Martin Company.

With the substantial regular Martin contract, Roy knew it was imperative to set up a tight control system and that meant more manpower. He began hiring again and boosted Sunbank's employee roster to twenty-five. It did indeed seem as though Roy had overcome the major hurdles and finally had a viable business on his hands.

It was during this time that Roy struck up a friendship with his partner's foreman, a man named Leonard Hauer. Leonard came to Sunbank in November, 1959. Today he is still working for Sunbank, although officially retired for several years. Unfortunately, Leonard's wife died at about the time he retired, and retirement alone was not what he had in mind. Now Leonard comes in each morning to open up the tool cage and help younger workers set up the machinery.

After watching Leonard work, Roy knew he was one of the best machinists he had ever seen. Leonard had risen to the top of the various grades of machinists to be a tool and die maker.

Over the next twenty-five years with Sunbank, Leonard Hauer would design many special tools for Roy's various machine shops and come up with a number of time and money-saving innovations for the production lines. His keen understanding of mechanical engineering was to help Roy "pull the fat out of the fire" on a number of occasions.

But at Sunbank the situation with Roy's new partner was not improving. It was getting worse. While Roy kept rambling along at his usual hundred hours or more a week, his partner made it abundantly clear he had no intention of putting in such long hours to build the business.

Finally, Roy confronted the inevitable. One of the partners would have to buy the other out. His partner agreed. The only snag in all this was that Roy only had a few thousand dollars in savings and bankers still thought he was too young to risk loaning him the money. The upshot of this was that Roy's partner said if Roy couldn't raise the money then he would buy Roy out.

"At that stage there was little I could do but go ahead and sell my share of Sunbank," explains Roy.

They agreed on a final price and Roy's partner promptly paid him half the amount with the balance to be paid in one year.

"Then I walked away fat, dumb and happy," says Roy. "But it sure didn't last long."

Roy took his new-found wealth and headed east for the beautiful Ozark Mountains of Arkansas. He had decided to buy a ranch and settle down to devote some time to his wife and two young daughters, Virginia and Nancy. From boyhood he had wanted his own ranch and he tackled the remodeling with the same enthusiasm and hard work he had put into Sunbank Electronics. But it was not to be. Six months after his arrival in Arkansas, Roy received a telegram from his ex-partner.

"Need help badly at Sunbank. Come back right away," the telegram read.

Roy telephoned his former partner. His partner had brought in a team of managers to run the business when Roy left. They had run the company into a deep hole. Sunbank was now one hundred thousand dollars in the red and digging deeper every day. Without Roy's immediate help, his ex-partner pleaded, not only would he not receive the other half of the money owed him, but in all likelihood Sunbank Electronics would fall into bankruptcy.

No matter how much he was enjoying his new life at the ranch, Roy could not sit by and watch his own creation destroyed through mismanagement. He agreed to return to California and talk to his ex-partner.

Roy admits this was a very "low point" in his life. He had begun to realize what a great opportunity he had with Sunbank, and to also realize he had not handled it well. Filled with anger and indecision, Roy went to a park in Burbank and sat down to think things over. He came very close to getting the next plane back to Arkansas.

"Then I realized that was not very smart," says Roy. "Here was the business I knew and the alternative was to go back to Arkansas and be a roofer and rancher. I knew I could do something with Sunbank. It didn't take very long to make a final decision. I had to get involved even though I knew it would put a lot of pressure on my home life.

Roy went to a luncheon meeting with the "committee" of managers. This meeting confirmed his worst fears. He told his ex-partner that if he continued to listen to this "committee," Sunbank would be two hundred thousand dollars in the hole within a short time.

The situation needing most urgent attention was sales. Roy's disappointment was bitter when he discovered that one of the reasons for falling sales was that Sunbank customers were receiving sub-standard parts. Roy called every customer on the list, informed them that he was back on the job and personally promised them there would be no more problem with quality.

At the end of that first week, Roy was made general manager. His first action was to fire the accountant and quality control manager of the so-called "committee," whose efforts had created the emergency in the first place. He placed Leonard Hauer in charge of production and personally took charge of the company.

It took Roy ten hard months to get Sunbank back on an even keel and out of financial difficulties. But there was a price to pay for that on the distaff side. His marriage disintegrated into a divorce. His wife, Patricia, had long felt she was on the losing end of a competition between herself and Roy's ambition. His return to Sunbank just confirmed for her that she had lost.

"In all honesty," Roy admits, "I look back on myself as I was then and I just don't think any woman alive could have put up with me. I was pretty much single-minded about my goals for success and I find it hard to lay any blame on Patricia for the failure of that marriage. I was putting in late hours most of the time and always on the road somewhere making sales calls."

Having been abandoned by his own parents made it doubly difficult for Roy when it came to custody of his two daughters. It was decided they would live with their mother, but this did not sit well with Roy. He loved his daughters deeply, but had little understanding of the needs and fears of little girls. With his heavy workload at Sunbank, he saw no alternative but to agree that his daughters stay with their mother. Later, when the chance came to gain custody of the girls, he jumped at it.

At Sunbank, Roy found his partner had not been substantially changed by his experience and Roy had no desire to continue the lion's share of the work as general manager, with his ex-partner as president and owner. Once again he faced his ex-partner with an ultimatum: either he find a buyer for the company or personally take over management of the company. But if he did take over, Roy said firmly, he was not to call on Roy again.

Roy would have jumped at the chance to buy back the company, but what money he had was tied up in the ranch in Arkansas and banks were still not interested in giving him financing. "When I came up with the buyer for Sunbank, it just seemed a better way to go," says Roy.

Wisely, his ex-partner opted for selling. The buyer was Knapic Electro-Physics Inc., a member of the Texas multi-millionaire, Jim Ling, corporate family.

The management of Knapic could see that Roy Coats was absolutely vital to the operation and quickly offered him full control as general manager with attractive stock options if he agreed to stay with Sunbank. Roy agreed, mainly because the offer was too good to refuse, but partly and significantly for the future, he really did not want to abandon his own creation again to the "bright ideas" of managers without any experience of what the business was all about.

Knapic felt good about the arrangement, as well as they should. In two years under Roy Coats' leadership, Sunbank Electronics would be rated the youngest (by average age of employees) company in California to gross over one million dollars in annual sales.

But Knapic also underestimated Roy Coats. Roy was basically an independent entrepreneur at heart and totally unsuited to being another cog in a corporate heirarchy — no matter what title he was given.

12
HIGH IN THE SADDLE

A new decade had begun. The start of what would later be called The Angry Sixties. For Roy Coats it was to be a decade of accomplishment, spiced with some high-risk gambles and some hard living.

President Eisenhower was seventy years old in 1960, had just come back from a world tour and there was talk of disarmament. The United States and Japan had signed the first treaty of mutual cooperation and security. Unemployment was on the way down, per capita income was on the way up. Peace had returned to the labor front after a crippling 116-day steel strike, which ended January 5th. Detroit turned out its best performance since 1955.

But events were speeding up — a foretaste of what was to come when it would seem to many people that events were moving so fast they were totally out of control. Eisenhower had a Civil Rights bill in the Congressional hopper as the year began, but the first lunch counter sit-in started in January. A whole new protest movement had been born.

Richard Nixon was the Republican front-runner, pledged to the "high road" and a refutation of the label "Tricky Dicky" that the media had given him. Meanwhile, against all odds, a Democrat called John Fitzgerald Kennedy was mobilizing support for what he called The New Frontier, as he criss-crossed the nation. On May 1st, a U-2 spy plane piloted by Francis Gary Powers was shot down over Russia and Premier Krushchev had a field day embarrassing the Administration. In the Buenos Aires suburb of San Fernando, four men kidnapped a slight, graying, hollow-cheeked factory worker and took him to Israel. His name was Adolf Eichmann.

That first year of the decade, 1960, also saw Hurricane Donna slash through Puerto Rico and into the southeastern part of the nation. The most destructive and vicious tropical storm since 1886. In the Congo, madness and bloodshed reigned as civil war erupted. In the United Nations, Soviet Premier Krushchev took off his shoe to thump on a desk. Fidel Castro came to New York and turned the town on its ear with his gun-toting body guards and extemporaneous speeches. Jimmy Hoffa, street-tough boss of the Teamsters Union, was wriggling out of income tax, wiretapping and bribery charges, unaware he would soon have Bobby Kennedy on his tail.

The nation mourned the death of The King — Clark Gable — in November, while filming *The Misfits* with Marylin Monroe. Sputniks were bounding up into space with regularity. Newly-formed NASA set its sights on manned space flight. By October that year it had five Mercury man-carrying capsules at Cape Canaveral, with manned orbital flights planned for the following year. It was now the fourth year of the space race and finally America was in the ball game for real.

Riding on the coat-tails of the aerospace boom was Sunbank Electronics. Roy Coats was twenty-five and Chief Executive Officer of the company he had founded with eight thousand dollars. He had gathered around him a loyal crew of men his own age or younger. What they lacked in business experience they more than made up for in enthusiasm and hard work.

Roy took a look at the growing expense and time involved in traveling around the country to service accounts. He decided it was time Sunbank had its own private plane and, true to character, took flying lessons. Roy went to groundschool at the Whiteman Air Park in Pacoima, just west of Burbank. His teacher was Don Brant, a former B-29 bomber pilot. Roy proved an apt pupil and after ten hours in the air with Brant, made his first solo flight. Flying proved to be not only a tremendous business asset. It was all very much in keeping with his current life style — work hard and play hard.

Roy's rambunctious lifestyle had been crimped somewhat during the early start-up period of Sunbank Electronics. Basically through lack of time and money. With Sunbank back on the rails again, Roy resumed his hard living ways. He took up water skiing, becoming very close with his cousin, William Lee (Buzz) Coats, who was then on his way to becoming a well-known speedboat racer until a racing accident ended his life prematurely.

"We would spend a lot of time driving or flying to the Colorado River," Roy explains. "We'd play hard all weekend, get drunk and disorderly, then drive 285 miles home on a Sunday afternoon. Sometimes it was with our wives, and sometimes it wasn't," Roy admits. There was also some mutual commiseration between Roy and Buzz over their marital problems. Like Roy, Buzz had brought a young bride home on discharge from the military service but both marriages were fast disintegrating.

The one stable influence in Roy's life continued to be Aunt Claudia, who had more than her own share of the Coats clans' wild and fearless ways. As Roy describes it, at that time "I was ready to try anything on a given day." And so was Aunt Claudia.

For instance, Roy and Buzz were driving Aunt Claudia to Texas one weekend to see her brother, Richard Coats. Heading east past San Bernardino on Highway 10 (that was before it became a freeway) Aunt Claudia announced she was hungry and wanted to eat. They were near the small town of Redlands. Roy wanted to at least get as far as Indio in the less heavily traveled San Bernardino County area before stopping. But once Aunt Claudia had made a decision, nothing could dissuade her.

"I'm hungry now, you little bastard!" she growled.

Roy knew there was no point in arguing further. He pulled up at a small restaurant. It was Friday evening and the restaurant was besieged with customers. The lineup for tables snaked through the restaurant foyer and out through the front door. There was a touch of actress in Aunt Claudia that took very little to bring out. In the past Roy had seen her put on a very convincing imitation of someone having a fit. As they walked up to the restaurant, Roy on one side of Aunt Claudia and Buzz on the other, Roy whispered to her.

"When we get up close to the door, throw one of your epileptic fits and see if we can't get a table a little faster."

"Alright," she replied gruffly, a gleam of mischief in her bright blue eyes. She then half-slumped between them so they had to hold her upright by her arms.

"Let us through here," Roy commanded. "This poor woman is having a fit!"

Tom Worthington with his horse

"Arraaawaaaa......!" yelled Aunt Claudia and the waiting crowd opened up instantly before them. By now, Roy and Buzz were literally half-dragging Aunt Claudia inside the restaurant and both were having a very hard time to keep a straight face.

The hostess was completely unnerved. She showed them to an empty booth immediately, then stood back almost ten feet from the table and nervously flipped the menus on the table, afraid the wild looking woman was about to have another uncontrollable spasm.

The food arrived with startling rapidity. Once in a while, Roy would whisper to Aunt Claudia, "Give them a little shot just for effect, Aunt Claudia."

Without batting an eye, she let loose with another "Arraawaaa..."

This was necessary because by now both Roy and Buzz were almost having fits themselves trying to control their laughter. Roy kept putting his head beneath the table so as not to give the game away.

With the meal over, they exited the restaurant, then all three broke into laughter as they walked towards their car.

"The incredible thing was she would do something like that with a totally straight face," Roy recalls. "I'm usually pretty good at keeping a straight face but she cracked me up so badly I just about died laughing. My sides ached for the next 300 miles."

Through his business, Roy made a number of close friends. Naturally enough, they tended to be highly individual men, like Roy, who also believed in hard work and sometimes even harder play. One such friend was Tom Worthington, the owner of an aluminum foundry not far from Sunbank's facility in Burbank.

Imagine Buffalo Bill reincarnated and running a foundry in Burbank, California, and you have Tom Worthington. Dressed in the well-cut Western clothes he has worn all of his life, his mane of gray hair cascades in elegant waves down past his shoulders from beneath a wide Stetson hat. A genuine throw-back — tough, ornery, fiercely independent.

When he first met Worthington, Roy was twenty-two and Worthington was in his fifties. Today, Tom is well into his seventies but still works every day and conducts a roaring social life that any thirty-year-old would envy. He is a man who resolutely refuses to think old.

As two self-made men from poor childhoods, it was natural they would become friends. Worthington was born in Nebraska. Like Roy, he received minimal education and came to California as a young boy. He apprenticed to a foundry until he had learned every single aspect of the trade, including the difficult lost-wax process, then struck out on his own.

The lost-wax process is used to make castings of high

precision. Liquid wax is injected into a steel die and allowed to cool. The wax pattern is removed from the die and used to make a mold. The patterns are dipped into a plaster-like material until covered with a thin coating. After the coating dries, it forms a hard finish that will not melt when molten metal is poured into the mold. The pattern is then heated in a furnace to melt the wax from inside of the plaster shell. The wax runs out, leaving a very precise mold into which molten metal is poured. When cooled, the mold is broken away from the finished casting.

Roy believes Worthington to be one of the best foundry operators in the business.

"The man is a perfectionist," Roy enthuses — another trait they both hold in common. "His quality control is so damn tough you will never, never get a flawed casting from that foundry."

Roy had heard mention of Worthington during his days at Pacific Automation. When he started Sunbank Electronics, Roy called Worthington's office and said he needed some castings made for his accessories.

"I was looking out my front window in the old Burbank Boulevard building," Roy recalls, "when a long white Cadillac drove up. Out stepped this son of Wild Bill Cody in boots, genuine Stetson hat and all the trimmings, just as neat as a pin. He walked right in as though he owned the place and gave it a real good once-over, as though wondering how he would ever make money from this shoestring outfit."

Roy showed Worthington the drawings and told him how many castings he needed. All Worthington said during the whole visit was "Uh huh" and left.

"And as I recall," says Roy, "I got that order ahead of schedule." They were friends from that day on.

Tom Worthington is the kind of man you either accept as he is, warts and all, or not at all. Indeed, many of Roy's friends couldn't understand why Roy chose to be friends with what to them appeared to be an extremely irascible, uninhibited, "hell-bound" and high handed individual. That Worthington was also a dedicated and long-time connoisseur of scotch whiskey didn't help matters.

"What I admire in Tom is his keen intelligence," counters Roy. "He has a talent for looking directly into the heart of a situation and identifying the real factors, plus he has a pride in the quality of his work and the capacity and desire to work and play hard."

Just by itself, that summation of his friend's qualities say a lot more about Roy Coats than is readily apparent. It illustrates what others have said over the years about Roy — that he has the ability to look through a situation, to see below the surface of things. Through his own experiences and nature, Roy found at an early age that outward appearance and "right conduct" can sometimes have little to do with someone's real worth as a human being.

Beneath Worthington's "larger than life" antics, Roy discerned an intelligence and expertise he could learn from. And most important — a man who worked hard and was proud of the quality of that work. Those are qualities Roy has always respected and strived for himself.

As a result, a special relationship developed between them. Indeed, there were many times when Worthington had a full head of steam that Roy was virtually the only person he would listen to. Many a man, misjudging the nature beneath those wavy gray locks, had only come to a true realization when he found himself on the floor staring up at Worthington's size twelve boots.

Roy vividly remembers one of a number of calls he received over the years to come and "handle" a situation involving Worthington "at play." The call was from a bar that Roy and Worthington frequented on a regular basis those days. Worthington, he was told, was terrorizing the bar. He had cornered three customers and if Roy didn't come right away the police would be called.

"So I drove over to the bar," says Roy, smiling, "and sure enough Tom was yelling at three customers he had herded into a corner — he was holding a chair on them like a lion tamer."

Roy strolled over to Worthington and quietly told him to put the chair down and "leave those poor people alone." To everyone's relief, Worthington complied. "Without another word, Tom set the chair down and allowed me to lead him away," Roy adds.

"That's just his style," Roy says to people who complain about Worthington's fondness for riding "high in the saddle."

"We are very good friends and I wouldn't have him any

Tom Worthington loves automobiles — here with his Rolls Royce

other way. I really admire his capacity to live life and enjoy it to the fullest."

Another close associate in those early days was Andy Allen, then on his way to becoming Roy's right-hand man at Sunbank. Roy had offered Aunt Claudia the use of the ranch in Arkansas. She thought it was a grand idea and moved there in short order. When Roy took Allen with him on a visit to Aunt Claudia at the ranch in Arkansas, Roy told Allen not to take any notice of Aunt Claudia's fiery manner.

On a previous visit to the ranch, she had greeted Roy with: "We need some stock on this ranch." So Roy dutifully went to a local sale barn and bought forty heifers and two bulls.

Shortly after Roy and Andy arrived at the ranch, Roy could tell that something was niggling at Aunt Claudia.

"We'd better brand these damn calves," she finally told him. "These Arkies gonna steal them if we don't."

Roy had also primed Andy Allen about the mutual game of teasing and the practical jokes they constantly played on one another. He winked at Andy and they both dutifully went to the corral to start branding. Without horses they had to bulldog the big heifer calves to the ground. One would hold the animal down while the other put on the brand.

Aunt Claudia watched the branding from the porch with a critical eye. Roy knew something was bothering her. Finally, she left the porch and moved towards the corral. It alarmed Roy how slowly she moved. Aunt Claudia had emphysema but he hadn't realized until then how serious it was. It seemed to take her about fifteen minutes to slowly hobble her way to the corral. Then she stood by the fence and watched them closely.

"You're branding them too damn low," she snapped.

Roy grabbed another heifer. This time he put the brand higher on the hip.

"That brand is too damn low," she yelled. At that moment the heifer took the opportunity of Roy's distraction to kick him in the side, roll free, and take off with only half the brand on.

"For Christ's sake, Aunt Claudia, why don't you go back to the house and let me get on with the branding?" Roy said, rubbing the sore place where the heifer had kicked him.

Aunt Claudia suddenly scowled at Roy as though he was still a small boy. With eyes blazing, she turned and ran towards the house like a young girl — in contrast to her labored shuffle down to the corral.

"You're a little son-of-bitch," she yelled over her shoulder. "And you're not getting any lunch either!"

Roy and Andy both collapsed in the dirt with laughter. Another Aunt Claudia story was about to make the rounds at Sunbank when Andy and Roy returned.

By 1961, Knapic's Sunbank Division was turning in quite a performance. New territories and accounts were coming on board almost daily as Roy piled up hundreds of hours of flying time and tens of thousands of miles driving.

In the nation as a whole there was a sense of new beginnings and new horizons with the inauguration of John Kennedy in January that year. It seemed we had nothing to look forward to but the best, either on the ground or in outer space. What 1961 turned out to be, though, was a year of trial for the President and the nation.

At the University of Georgia, it would take the full might of the federal government to get a young black girl and youth inside to enroll. Fidel Castro was handed a propaganda bonanza when the ill-conceived and badly fumbled Bay of Pigs invasion of Cuba by Cuban exiles proved a disastrous failure. The infamous Berlin Wall went up. There were new concerns about events in Laos and, more ominous still, the first small steps towards United States involvement in Vietnam.

Russia put the first man into Space April 12th and on May 15th we sent Alan Shepard up in Freedom 7. On May 25th, President Kennedy told Congress he would like to see the Stars and Stripes on the moon before the decade ended. The already booming aerospace industry was about to go into overdrive.

That July, 1961, Roy felt that business was going well enough he could afford to visit the ranch in Arkansas. Although he didn't know it at the time, Andy Allen was about to become involved in what came to be known at Sunbank as The Great Adventure.

Roy had bought himself a Caterpillar tractor-dozer for use at the ranch and intended to haul it out there himself on board an old 2½-ton truck he had also purchased. When he asked Andy Allen if he would care to give him a hand on the trip, Andy readily agreed. Its sounds like fun, he told Roy.

"We'll probably have to take an extra day or two off work before we get back," said Roy casually.

Roy was aware that the huge tractor was really more than the old truck could comfortably handle but — in those days — he was used to running on the edge.

"Don't worry about it, Andy," said Roy, when he saw Andy nervously eyeing the huge tractor mounted on the back of the battered truck.

"We won't push the truck too hard and everything will work out just fine. You'll see," he added by way of encouragement.

Their route went through Phoenix then Salt River Canyon to Socorro, New Mexico and east to pick up old Route 66 for Oklahoma and Arkansas.

Roy stopped in Phoenix to say hello to Eakle Colliflower. He had an inkling that the rear bearings on the truck might be feeling the pressure, so Eakle's assistant at the gas station removed the bearings, said they looked in good shape and put them back.

Roy said his farewell to Eakle and set off for Salt River

Canyon. About a mile-and-a-half from Eakle's gas station, one of the rear bearings froze solid. Eakle's inexperienced assistant had forgotten to grease the bearings before reinstalling them on the rear wheels.

It was the following morning before new bearings could be found and put in and the journey continue. The truck got as far as the New Mexico border before the rear axle of the truck broke in two. The metal of the axle had crystallized from the heat generated by the frozen wheel bearing.

Andy Allen, city born and bred, spent a very restless night on the edge of the desert while Roy hitchhiked to the nearest town for a tow-truck. It was midnight by the time the tow-truck deposited the truck and Roy and Andy in a small town. Because of the holiday weekend, all the hotels and motels in town were full. Undaunted, Roy said they would sleep out and introduced a wary Andy to his first experience of "sleeping out" in an old camper shell on the back of a truck in a used car lot. So far the trip had definitely not been the kind of "fun" Andy expected.

The next morning, Roy located a mechanic to work on the truck then told Andy they would have to catch a ride into Phoenix to locate a new rear axle for the truck.

By now, Andy's faith in Roy was wearing thin. "Hell, Andy said, pointing to a hitchhiker standing by the side of the road. "I've been watching that guy for two hours and he hasn't got a ride. What makes you think we can?" he added sceptically.

"That's because he doesn't know how to hitchhike," Roy said quietly.

Roy took an unconvinced Andy into a nearby restaurant for breakfast. Roy's technique was simple but effective. He sat where he could see cars pulling up at the restaurant and thus know in which direction they were traveling. When a likely prospect came, Roy struck up a friendly conversation, expressed interest in where the couple had been and where they were going. Of course, the couple in turn asked Roy the same questions so he could casually explain how he was stranded and trying to get to Phoenix to get a new axle. Within 15 minutes, Roy and a surprised Andy were on their way to Phoenix. The hitchhiker still stood hopefully by the side of the road.

That night they slept at Eakle Colliflower's house. Next

Roy & Andy Allen at Andy's wedding

morning, Roy located a suitable axle in an automobile junkyard. Roy, Eakle and the contrite helper worked straight through the rest of the day; before evening the truck was back on the road and heading for New Mexico.

With such a heavy and bulky load, driving was something of a strain and Andy was now looking forward to a speedy end of the trip. They made quite good time through Arizona and New Mexico, but near the town of McClain, Texas, the front wheel bearings burned out.

A new set of bearings was installed, but Roy knew the excessive weight had damaged the bearing races. He bought an extra set of bearings just in case.

They made another 150 miles before the bearings gave out again. Andy was not mechanically minded, but Roy put him through a crash course over the next thousand miles as they stopped by the side of the road to put in new bearings every 150 miles. After the fourth or fifth time, they had it down to twenty minutes or less.

By this time they were bone weary. They took turns sleeping in the small truck cab while the other drove to make up the lost time. One night they pitched their sleeping bags on the sidewalk in front of a parts store to make sure they would be awakened the minute the store opened.

Dusk was approaching as they lumbered along the highway from Oklahoma City. As the truck bounced heavily over railroad tracks there was a tremendous crash.

Roy pulled the truck over and told Andy to check around and see if something had fallen off. Andy checked the wheels and springs and looked at the huge tractor. He could see nothing missing. Roy presumed it was probably the steel bed of the truck popping when they hit the tracks.

Thirty miles down the road a tire blew, something that had been happening with irritating regularity. Roy got out and went to the back of the truck for the spare tire. It was then he saw the entire tailgate was missing.

"Hell, Andy," Roy grumbled, "the whole damn tailgate flew off back there. What did you look at when you walked around?"

They changed the tire and drove back the thirty miles to the railroad crossing. By then it was completely dark without even the moonlight to help them. Roy took one side of the road, and Andy the other, and both began fumbling in the dark for the tailgate.

Roy heard the happy sounds of a wedding party in progress coming from a nearby house. Without mentioning it to Andy, he ambled over to the house to inquire if anyone had seen the missing tailgate.

The people inside had no knowledge of the tailgate, but they insisted Roy come inside for coffee and a piece of cake.

Enjoying his coffee and cake, surrounded by a group of local ladies, Roy happened to glance at the window. He could see Andy's eyes glaring at him in astonishment and fury through the glass. Then Andy turned away and stomped back to the truck.

Roy finished his cake and coffee, thanked the ladies for their kind hospitality and set off after the irate Andy.

Andy was tired and upset at not having noticed the missing tailgate in the first place. When Roy got to the truck he began to rage at Roy.

"Here I am," Andy fumed, "worn out, stumbling around the prairie in the dark and what are you doing?" Sitting down drinking coffee and eating cake!"

Roy suppressed the urge to laugh, which would only have

infuriated Andy even more. Gradually, Roy calmed him down, then both went back to search for the tailgate. They found it finally and reattached it to the truck.

The remainder of the trip was a succession of flat tires and worn front wheel bearings. Resigned to his fate now, Andy played his harmonica when not driving. One mile from Roy's ranch the second of four back tires blew without a spare tire, they crawled the last mile to the ranch leaving a trail of shredded tires behind them.

By the time Roy and Andy got back to Los Angeles, they had been on the road two-and-a-half weeks instead of the five days originally envisioned. If nothing else, it says volumes about Roy Coats' persistence. As for Andy Allen, his only comment to Roy was short but heartfelt:

"Roy, I don't want any more of these damn adventures!"

13

TURBULENT YEARS

The early 1960s were turbulent years for the world at large and for America in particular. This turbulence was reflected in Roy Coats' own experiences during those years, but through it all he kept fortifying Sunbank's strength and adding to his own store of business expertise.

In 1962, the situation worsened in Vietnam, Laos and Berlin. The nation had something to cheer about, though, when John Glenn Jr., made the first manned orbital flight on February 20th and President Kennedy pushed a space budget through Congress of over five billion dollars.

May 28th that year became known as Black Monday. The economy turned sour, panic selling swept the Exchanges and the value of holdings for seventeen million stockholders plunged by $20.8 billion. Incredibly, the market firmed the next day, and President Kennedy faced down U.S. Steel and its proposed six dollars a ton price hike for steel and the economy steadied.

In other areas Kennedy was having a rough time. Congress filibustered his amendments in the Civil Rights area. The vortex of Vietnam sucked in another thousand military advisors, along with Marine Corps helicopters and fighter planes. Kennedy sent four thousand soldiers into Thailand as Laotian fighting intensified. Martin Luther King Jr., was gaining national attention as he continued to get himself arrested all over the South.

That summer, Soviet freighters churned the waters off Cuba, loaded with long-range missiles that could blow away American cities. On October 16th the attention of the world was centered on the Cuban Missile Crisis and for thirteen long days the world teetered fearfully on the edge of thermonuclear war. President Kennedy put everything on the line with troops on standby for invasion in Florida and a quarantine line of U.S. Navy ships around Cuba. At the last minute, twenty Soviet vessels and a submarine stopped dead in the water just before the quarantine line. Soviet Premier Khrushchev backed down and the missiles were removed from Cuba.

Nixon ran for governor of California that year and lost badly. He took it badly, too, saying "You won't have Nixon to kick around anymore," declaring he was bowing out of politics for good. Jack Paar quit the popular "Tonight Show" and NBC picked an unknown named Johnny Carson to replace him.

The Dodgers' Maury Wills stole 104 bases that season, breaking Ty Cobbs forty-seven-year one season mark of 96. The amazing Mets, with Casey Stengel at the helm, set a record of 120 losses and 40 wins, while the Yanks took the World Series four games to three from the San Francisco Giants. Two new faces came to national attention that year. One was a rookie pro golfer, Jack Nicklaus, 22 years old, who beat Arnold Palmer for the U.S. Open title by three strokes. In college football, a sophomore quarterback named Roger Staubach led Navy to a 34-14 win over Army.

Sunbank Electronics, Inc., posted over one million dollars in gross sales in 1962. A remarkable achievement for a company run by a twenty-seven-year-old chief executive, where most of the employees were the same age or younger.

It had taken Roy a great deal of hard work and a lot of time away from home and his two young daughters to reach that point; but the need for a stable home environment for his daughters was constantly in his thoughts.

One obvious solution was to remarry. Roy had been seeing an attractive young woman, named Joy, recently divorced with a young son of her own. They had originally met when she was a secretary at Pacific Automation. Joy had an easy-going style and some understanding of business pressures. Roy found he could talk to her about his work and plans for the future.

"There is no doubt I chose an entirely different type of person from my first wife," says Roy. "But the truth is...I didn't spend enough time getting to know her. She was a very desirable young woman and that seemed to be enough at the time."

They were married in Las Vegas in 1962. This time, Roy

believed he could establish a more meaningful relationship than had been the case in his first marriage.

As turbulent as events were in 1962, they were nothing compared to 1963. We now had 16,000 American military advisors fighting in Vietnam. The U.S. Navy's pride and joy — the nuclear submarine U.S. Thresher — went to the bottom with 129 men on board. President Kennedy received a tumultuous welcome in Berlin. At home, racial tension spread from the South to New York, Chicago, Philadelphia and Los Angeles. There were riots in Alabama and South Carolina. Martin Luther King Jr., led the march on Washington and gave his "I have a dream..." speech.

Attorney General Bob Kennedy closed down the infamous Rock — the island prison of Alcatraz. Minimum wage went up to $1.25 an hour and, on television, an ex-mobster called Joe Valachi spilled the beans on La Cosa Nostra and the crime syndicate families he claimed ran the nation's underworld.

On November 22nd, President John F. Kennedy was shot in Dallas and a wave of shock and grief swept the nation and the world. Lyndon Johnson assumed the office of President and gradually the country put the pieces back together. Just for a change, the Yankees lost the World Series that year, 4-0 to the Dodgers. The Mets, of course, finished last again — by a wide margin.

At Sunbank Electronics, Inc., sales continued to hold to an upward trend, but trouble was brewing with Knapic Electro-Physics, the parent company. Over the previous two years, Knapic had lost $3½ million and was siphoning off Sunbank's cash flow to keep them afloat.

This steady rising financial drain threatened to ruin Sunbank and therefore Roy took matters into his own hands and flew to Dallas to see Jim Ling. Ling was one of the prime movers and shakers in the aviation industry and had put together the Ling-Temco-Vought conglomerate. Ling was also owner of Electro Science Investors, the Dallas-based holding company which owned Knapic and a number of other companies.

Roy said to Ling that while he personally didn't care if Knapic went broke because of poor management, there seemed no good reason to destroy a promising and profitable operation like Sunbank in the process. Ling agreed and gave Roy permission to refuse Knapic's demands for cash. Almost

Joe & Nita Wittman in front of King Air with Roy & Laura

in passing, Ling expressed his appreciation to Roy that Sunbank was the only profitable company he had in California. He asked Roy if he would survey his other California companies and present his recommendations on what should be done with them. Roy said he would.

In California, Roy shut down the cash flow to Knapic and toured the nine other companies in the Ling empire. What he saw was disaster in the making and he didn't mince any words in his report to Ling: "Close down eight of the companies immediately," he said, "take whatever losses are necessary and greatly reduce operations in the remaining company until it is back on a profitable footing."

"Well, they didn't do it," Roy recalls, "and over the next two or three years lost seven or eight million dollars!"

While Knapic floundered, Roy criss-crossed the nation on sales trips, piloting a small rented plane, as he had been doing since first taking flying lessons in 1960. Roy was a competent pilot, but by his own admission felt he was far from being a really good pilot.

In 1963 Roy met a flyer by the name of Joe Wittman. Wittman had flown for Pan Am for a number of years before moving on to pilot for private companies in the San Francisco area. After a flight or two with Wittman, Roy realized how far he still had to go to become a good pilot.

Wittman undertook to improve Roy's understanding of aircraft and flying and they formed a friendship and mutual respect which has lasted to this day.

"Joe taught me how to operate an aircraft so that the passengers are as comfortable as possible, while still getting the maximum performance from the plane," says Roy. "It is the kind of experience that only comes through true flight experience and a natural talent for flying that all great pilots seem to possess."

Wittman's conviction that a pilot should know and understand the function of each and every piece of gear and instrumentation on an aircraft was in tune with Roy's methodical approach to business decisions — a major factor in his success. Today, Roy never flies without a thorough preflight inspection of the aircraft, from the tires up. In 1963, the careful consideration of all options and consequences was fast becoming an integral part of Roy's business management philosophy. As such, it has become an important maxim in his formula for success.

"Learn all you can about a situation, both pro and con, before making a decision," Roy urges. "And don't be pressured by other people's consideration of time and urgency. Emergencies and poor decisions invariably result from a lack of careful planning or forethought," he adds.

As it turned out, it took a minimum of forethought on Roy's part to see that unless Knapic made a sudden and near-miraculous reversal of its downward plunge, Knapic and all connected with it would be faced with the spector of bankruptcy. As a subsidiary of Knapic, Sunbank Electronics would have to go down with the sinking ship.

Through no fault of his own or his company, Roy's tireless work and careful planning at Sunbank seemed as if it might be to no avail as Roy toasted in the New Year of 1964.

14
CHESTNUTS FROM THE FIRE

As 1964 rolled on it became obvious that nothing was going to stop Knapic Electro-Physics from sliding into bankruptcy and taking Sunbank Electronics with it. Indeed, it seemed the whole country was sliding downhill that year.

Despite an unprecedented forty-five of fifty-two pieces of President Johnson's legislation on civil rights, poverty and housing being passed by Congress (as Johnson called in markers from his time as Majority Leader), it seemed to most Americans a whole way of life was being torn apart.

It was the year of the "long hot summers" and the worst racial turmoil of the Sixties. That summer the bombing of North Vietnam began, following the controversial Gulf of Tonkin incident between U.S. destroyers and North Vietnamese gunboats. The Beatles arrived in America and came to national attention on the Ed Sullivan Show. Martin Luther King Jr., received the Nobel Peace Prize while, ironically, college campuses became centers of anarchy under sit-ins, picketing, draft card burnings, drugs, and violent political activism.

Moscow radio announced that on his own request "Mister Khrushchev" was to be relieved of his burdensome post as Soviet Premier. In Trenton, New Jersey, a dignified gray haired man of fifty-four came quietly out of the State Prison and went to work in the New York garment district. He was Charles (The Bug) Workman who had served twenty-nine years for the Murder Inc., massacre of Dutch Schultz and three of his henchmen in 1935 — the same year that Roy Coats was born.

Finally Knapic Electro-Physics filed for bankruptcy. As one of their divisions, Sunbank Electronics was included. As word spread, vendors wanted to cut off Sunbank's credit and some of Roy's employees, mindful of their own careers, began looking for other jobs and not paying very much mind to the work in front of them.

With Sunbank facing certain ruin if something wasn't done quickly, Roy flew to San Francisco to see the bankruptcy receivers. It took a lot of persuasion, but Roy managed to convince the hard-nosed receivers that the only way they would see a return on the Knapic losses was to sell off the Sunbank division to the highest bidder while there was still time.

By now sales had dropped at Sunbank from one million plus to around seven-hundred-thousand dollars, but still respectable enough to attract...potential investors. And attract them it did. A flood of prospective buyers trooped through the Sunbank plant, wanting to see every nook and cranny. Even with the sales decline, Sunbank still looked like a good risk, situated as it was in a highly specialized and growing aerospace market.

A high percentage of the would-be buyers expressed interest in buying Sunbank, but only if Roy would stay on as general manager. Roy made it very clear he had no interest in doing so. He told them plainly that he had no intention of ever again becoming "another man's pawn." One after another, the prospective buyers lost interest in Sunbank without Roy to manage it.

It soon became apparent to Roy that the only logical buyer was himself. It was almost a replay of the situation he found himself in five years earlier, when he proposed to his then-partner that one should buy the other out. Once again, Roy did not have the money and getting a loan was easier said than done.

Nor was it an easy decision to make. Roy had numerous doubts about being able once again to pull Sunbank back from the edge of ruin and (since Sunbank had now grown in size) the risk had increased proportionately. Then Roy's naturally competitive attitude came to the fore — the attitude that would become his own personal motto: No Guts — No Glory. He would buy the company.

Roy sold his house and whatever else would bring a price and went to his friend, Tom Worthington the foundry owner.

"Roy came to me and said he could buy the company out from the bankruptcy court," Worthington recalls, "but that he'd need $150,000 to do it, and would I like to go in for a third? Well, truth to tell, I'd have jumped at the chance, but at the time I just didn't have the cash."

Roy went to the bank. This time they showed some interest, providing he could come up with co-guarantors agreeable to the bank. An old friend of Roy's agreed to co-sign the loan, and brought in one of his own friends as well. Both men became co-guarantors with Roy for a loan of $150,000 — the price Roy was going to offer for Sunbank. For doing so, each guarantor received a twenty percent share of the business. It took Roy five years to retire the loan and in that time his co-guarantors enjoyed a very healthy cash flow without ever having to actually put up any cash.

Roy took the offer of $150,000 to the receivers. After witnessing a parade of interested buyers who suddenly turned cold on the deal, they welcomed Roy's offer with open arms. Knapic Electro-Physics, however, was far from happy at the idea. They told the creditors they had offers from other buyers willing to pay a good deal more than $150,000 if only Roy would stay on as general manager.

"Hell no!" Roy told them emphatically, "If I'm going to run the company and have the responsibility for it, I'm going to own it or not be there. If you don't want me to put up the money and buy Sunbank then say so now and I'll leave."

At that point the bankruptcy referee stepped in. His first duty was to see that the creditors received some return on their losses and $150,000 cash now was better than any conditional promise. "Hold everything," the referee said. "We want the money."

"Sunbank was mine again," Roy remembers with satisfaction. "And right then and there I decided that never again would I get involved in a partnership deal. And I have not, to this day."

As the story goes, there are two empty golden thrones still waiting in heaven for the first two partners who died and still liked each other. It is a story Roy Coats and many other businessmen can get behind without any difficulty at all.

With Roy fully in control of Sunbank's destiny again, a shot of adrenalin-like enthusiasm ran through the company. They had weathered the storm of bankruptcy and now the brakes were off.

Roy still had a core of loyal employees. Like Roy, now twenty-nine, they were young and energetic and prepared to give their all to make Sunbank a success.

At that time, Sunbank consisted of one 11,000 square foot facility on Ontario Boulevard in Burbank, with an additional 8,000 square feet of leased space in a nearby building. It was a long way yet from being an empire, but it was enough to let Roy give full rein to his imaginative approach to selling and allow him to structure and expand the company in his own distinctive style.

The one quality Roy Coats has never lacked is initiative and no one was more aware of that than his competitors. Even so, Roy remained on friendly terms with the people he had worked with at Pacific Automation and their subsidiary, Glenair Incorporated — Roy's main competitor in connector accessories.

Shortly after regaining ownership of Sunbank, Roy was having a drink with some old friends from Pacific Automation and Glenair. The then chief executive of Glenair happened to be sitting at a nearby table. He came over to Roy and made a high-handed remark that over the years both he and his company have had good cause to regret.

"We're going to run you so damn far out of business you'll wish you had never left your ranch in Arkansas," he boasted to Roy in a loud voice.

It was a thoughtless remark in more ways than one in that it kicked Roy's already considerable incentive to succeed into overdrive.

"It was the best thing that could have happened to me at that time," Roy recalls. "For the next year, if I would normally make six calls a day, I would make twelve, just remembering that remark. And where I would normally work twelve hours, I'd work eighteen. That man gave me more incentive than any person I've ever come across. Not only was I determined that he wasn't going to run me out of business, but that he had better hang on tight to his own seat as well."

As it turned out, Pacific Automation soon had serious problems of its own. The company had been very successful with extremely rapid growth. It then went public at the height of the aerospace boom and the stock soared from ten to forty dollars a share. Then one of the chief stockholders abruptly sold all his stock and left the company. Pacific Automation went into a tailspin from which it never recovered.

The new president of Pacific Automation was so incensed by the abrupt pullout that he terminated the contract with the Glenair operation, with which the now departed major stockholder had close ties, and gave all the connector accessories business to Sunbank.

15
THE GREAT DIATOMACEOUS EARTH AND OTHER CAPERS

That first year of sole ownership in 1964 was a busy one for Roy and the company. It was also a year where the exhilaration of once again being in sole charge of his own destiny brought to flower Roy's inherent taste for risk and opportunities.

But better than most, Roy knew how to evaluate risks. Typical was his decision in 1964 to establish his own in-house die-casting facility. Although the techniques of die-casting were new to him, Roy did know that Sunbank bought a lot of such services from outside companies. If the die-casting could be done in-house it would provide better quality control and lower cost — two key elements in Sunbank's success so far.

Nevertheless, to do so was a risk. Sunbank would have to drum up enough business to justify the large capital outlay. Some of Roy's key people thought the risk too great and urged Roy to back away from it.

But Roy, as usual, sweated all the details and decided the risk was well worth the potential return. It was another No Guts — No Glory situation. Better than his managers, Roy knew that getting more business was largely a matter of determination and hard work — qualities he had in abundance.

"One thing about Roy," says Max Tillman, a manufacturer's representative at the time "is that while he does gamble a lot with horseshoe games, pool and golf, he never gambles with business. Roy feels anyone who does so is crazy. You have got to get the edge."

Getting the edge, as Ernest Baum had demonstrated to Roy many times in the past, meant a very careful consideration of all the options and consequences of any decision. This had become Roy's own Golden Rule.

"Obviously, you have to investigate and look into the ramifications of what you're proposing to do," Roy explains, "but once you've made up your mind that a particular course of action is a good thing, then don't back off. Don't be afraid of it. Having weighed all the factors and come to a decision based on the facts, plus your own intuition, you then have to assume the attitude that you *will* prevail. That you *will* move forward with it and not let it slip away, or yourself become weary of making it happen."

Roy firmly believes such an attitude applies not only in business but to life in general. Each individual must make a decision that they are either happy and going to make the best of it, or are not happy and going to make a change in their life.

"To spend your life in a job or situation that is meaningless to you, just for reasons of security or because you don't have the guts to do what you really want to do in life, is a horrible way to spend one's existence," Roy declares. "Over the course of my business career I've encouraged many people to make such a decision and invariably they are a hundred times happier after doing so; and within a very few years are doing ten times better than they were before."

Roy weighed all the risks and the possible benefits of the investment and made up his mind. He would go ahead and set up an in-house die-casting operation.

That decision allowed Sunbank to increase its unit volume ten-fold without any decrease in quality and a considerable saving in manufacturing costs through tight in-house control. The die-casting division did so well, in fact, that later it became a separate subsidiary company of Sunbank under the name of Royal Die Casting, supplying not only Sunbank's needs but that of other companies as well.

In an industry based on service and quality, Roy now felt he had quality in hand. What he had to do now was not only deliver the best service, but make Sunbank stand out from the crowd — an individuality that would create that valuable word-of-mouth advertising no money can buy. It is a promotional sales hat Roy wore from the first day he started his own business and a hat he still wears to this day.

An example of imaginative promotion was the purchase of a neglected 1928 Rolls Royce Town Car — with the open driver's compartment in front and the enclosed passenger area behind. In those days, Roy still liked a game of pool and slipped out for a game with his friend, Max Tillman, whenever time would allow. They were playing one afternoon, in one of their favorite Burbank watering holes, when one of Roy's engineers came in and mentioned an old Rolls Royce he had seen for sale.

"We went to look at it behind a garage," recalls Max Tillman. "It was shot, looked awful. We all laughed about it and went back to work." Then, about three that afternoon, Roy came into Max's office and told Max he had bought the car. "The hell you did," Max said to Roy.

Roy had already envisioned the elegant machine restored to its former glory. When Max and Roy put in a battery, the car fired up and ran well enough to take it for a drive. They soon found the clutch was in bad shape and took the car to a Rolls Royce dealer.

"It will be like cancer once you're into it," the dealer said. This was not happy news to Roy. He curtly told the dealer to close the car up and drove away.

A short time later, Roy heard of a talented young mechanic in North Hollywood. At first Roy was not impressed with the long-haired, scraggly looking kid. But the mechanic knew his business. He dove under the car and with a few hand adjustments had the clutch working perfectly.

"We hired a chauffeur and went out to celebrate," remembers Tillman. And celebrate they did. At one point in the evening, they sat the chauffeur in the back and drove him around from bar to bar.

"That kid mechanic knew the car pretty well," recalls Tillman. "Roy asked him if he thought he might be able to get it really running right. Well, that kid lit up like a Christmas tree."

With the help of Leonard Hauer, Roy's top tool and die maker, who fabricated parts too worn to be used or not available from the dealer, the car was completely rebuilt and professionally refinished. In gleaming black and maroon paint, it was truly an elegant and eye-catching automobile again, from her polished wire wheels to the crystal bud vase in the passenger compartment holding a fresh rose.

With the Rolls Royce restored, Roy now had a promotional sales instrument to help Sunbank "stand out from the crowd." As the aerospace industry had grown and become more sophisticated, so had the standards of quality control demanded by the aerospace companies from their sub-contractors. This meant a regular parade of prospective customers from aerospace companies to the Sunbank plant before orders were finalized.

Roy sent the Rolls Royce with chauffeur to pick up one of the customers arriving at nearby Burbank Airport. The customer was duly impressed and said so. After dinner with Roy, the car was turned over to the customer, complete with chauffeur, for the evening. Now the customer was really impressed.

It didn't take long for word of this "royal treatment" to spread throughout the industry. Requests began to pour into Sunbank and finally it got so out of hand with demands from customers for use of the Rolls that Roy had to reluctantly retire the car altogether. But during the time of its use, it created more good will and promotion for Sunbank than a professional public relations and promotion campaign costing many times the worth of the car.

The Rolls, by the way, still occupies a place of pride in the garage of Roy's Rainbow Ranch home in Paso Robles. No doubt one of these days she will be called into service again when an occasion presents itself.

It was these little extra touches — that added flair — that no doubt gave Roy the reputation for being "special" or "lucky." It is not a reputation Roy likes. It rankles him when people unconsciously try to dismiss what has been accomplished with foresight and hard work by calling him "lucky."

"As far as I'm concerned, no luck or special talent has been involved at all," Roy protests. "I simply had the determination to learn, the will to improve and a dedication to doing so in a logical, thoughtful way. Luck or opportunity does not occur out of a clear blue sky. It is made," he emphasizes. "What other people call luck is simply being able to recognize an opportunity when it comes along and then having the courage to go into action on that opportunity."

It is only natural in a book about one man's success that the emphasis should fall on successful actions and strategies. Equally important, though, is the ability to learn from one's mistakes — for mistakes there will be in the real world no matter how brilliant one is or how hard one tries to avoid them.

An inflexible pride which cannot admit to having made

a mistake is a terrible handicap to have in business or any other form of interrelationship. In order to learn from a mistake or bad decision one must admit there has been a mistake. Then one can look at it clearly and learn from the experience. To be in constant fear of making a mistake can paralyze one's ability to take risks and seize opportunities. Which brings us around again to No Guts — No Glory.

One scheme which did not turn out as planned came to be known among Roy's friends as the The Great Diatomaceous Earth Caper. It came about when Roy — ever eager to pursue opportunity — received an excited phone call from his uncle Richard Coats.

Richard Coats was blessed with an appealing sense of humor and a happy-go-lucky attitude towards life that completely disarmed people. With his puckish smile, round face and matching round stomach, he was a small town Falstaff with an endless supply of jokes and a genuine love for people. A plasterer by trade, Richard lived in an area where there was not enough work to support him. To supplement his income he painted houses and did odd jobs. He also developed a small business sideline making cement rings for use as watering troughs for cattle.

Richard made the rings in his backyard then sold them to ranchers. Mounted on a cement footing in the ground and connected to a water supply, they were virtually indestructible and can still be found in use in the Seymour Texas area.

There was also some of that Ernest Baum quality about Richard Coats, in that he was always looking for opportunities, and was a natural salesman. Roy used to watch him operate as he sold and traded fighting chickens, then still legal in that part of Texas.

It was while driving through Arizona on his way back to Seymour, after a visit to California, that Richard — his eyes "wide open" as usual — spotted a small "mountain" sticking out of the desert, as he described it. He stopped his car and went to investigate. He found what he had only hopefully expected — a huge mound of diatomaceous earth near the town of Duncan, Arizona.

Diatomaceous earth is an extremely fine talcum-like powder material composed of the decayed skeletons of countless minute planktonic organisms called diatoms. Millions of years ago, that part of Arizona had been part of an ocean floor that extended all the way into Montana. When some disaster overtook the area, causing the diatoms to die en masse, it so happened it occurred in immense localized clusters. The change in geology and climate over millions of years raised and dried these old ocean beds and now and then these mounds are exposed to view.

Diatomaceous earth (DE) is a remarkably efficient filtering agent and has become indispensible for filtering in breweries, dry cleaning plants and in the swimming pool industry. Lower grade DE cannot be used for these applications, but does find use as an oil soak and floor sweep material in gas stations and machine shops.

When Richard Coats got back to Seymour, he put a telephone call through to Roy.

"Boy oh boy, have I found it!" he said excitedly. It's sticking right out of the ground. I'm going to get a tractor and hammer mill and sacks... have you got somebody to bring along with you, Roy, because we ought to have at least four or five people to help us," Richard went on breathlessly.

Roy said he thought he knew someone who might be interested and that he would meet Richard in Duncan, Arizona.

Roy knew that his friend Max Tillman wasn't pleased with his current employer. When Roy explained what was going on, Max readily agreed to quit his job as salesman and manufacturer's representative and join in a three-way partnership. Roy and Max threw some tools and paper sacks into a truck and took off for Arizona and Uncle Richard's bonanza.

The excited trio met at a small motel in Duncan. At daylight the next morning they set off for the site. After considerable effort they got Uncle Richard's hammer mill and tractor unloaded and dragged the mill to the top of the "Mountain." All day they dug diatomaceous earth which, in its natural state, is like a soft rock. They put the earth through the hammer mill then loaded the fine powder into fifty pound sample sacks.

That evening, tired and dusty, they came down from the mound. Locals in Duncan referred to their truckloads of diatomaceous earth as "leachie" and made quiet remarks to each other about the "fool strangers digging leachie" out in the desert.

When they left Duncan, Roy had almost a ton of DE in

his truck and Uncle Richard had a full load in his own truck. They discussed how they would go about having the DE tested and the formation of a company to mine and sell the DE. Richard Coats said he would file a prospector's claim.

Back in California, Max Tillman wasted no time and soon had a laboratory test in hand stating that it was indeed commercial grade diatomaceous earth. Convinced now that a real fortune was in their hands, Roy formed a company called Reliable Products to mine and sell the DE, with Max Tillman as vice-president.

Roy sent Max to visit the huge diatomaceous earth mine run by Johns Manville near Santa Barbara, California, where giant scoops continually dig out and fill whole trainloads with DE for shipment all over the country.

With dreams of a similar future, Max Tillman opened an office on Victory Boulevard in Burbank and — good agressive salesman that he is — sold trainloads of DE for future delivery as soon as the mining equipment was in place.

Wanting to get further proof of the DE's effectiveness, Roy persuaded the owner of a dry cleaning plant in Sun Valley to use some of the DE they had brought back. The DE is used in the filtering system to clean the solvent. The owner's initial reaction to the product, and Roy's description of their find, was to ask if he could buy a piece of their DE mountain. Roy suggested they leave any such discussion until everything had been completely proven.

Meanwhile, Max Tillman and Richard Coats were selling truckloads to service stations to soak up oil. In the middle of all this frenzied activity, Roy received a call from the owner of the dry cleaning plant.

"You know boys," he said, "I'm having a little problem with this diatomaceous earth. When I mix it in fresh and turn on the pump it just does a wonderful job. But when I turn it off at night that earth doesn't stay up against the screen like it normally does. It falls off and next morning, when I turn on the pump, it's half an hour before the earth gets back up and covers the screen."

With sinking hearts, Roy and Max went back to the testing laboratory and demanded more tests. This time the test showed that although the earth was just good enough to squeak into the commercial grade, it just wasn't good

Roy & Max Tillman by the Beachcraft Baron

enough to do a proper job of industrial filtering, where the real commercial market lay.

It didn't take Roy very much time to work out that the only remaining market for the DE — as an oil soak for service stations — would not justify the costs of mining and trucking. The bonanza was regretfully over.

The mining venture had not worked out, but Roy liked the idea of a specialty products division within Sunbank. It appealed to his instincts as an entrepreneur. He decided to move Reliable Products into Sunbank and call it the Specialty Products Division, with Max Tillman as special projects manager.

For some years prior to this time, Roy had been an enthusiastic golfer. He took up the sport to improve his business dealings with customers, but had grown to love the game for its own sake. The first product the new division came up with was an attachment for golf carts that would measure the number of yards traveled as you went along. It seemed an easy and inexpensive way to monitor how far golfers were hitting their balls and a way to estimate the distance remaining to the hole from wherever you happened to be on the fairway.

After a great deal of development work and testing to try and overcome the variables of different surfaces and lengths and types of grass the unit had to operate over, Roy and Max realized the research and marketing costs still needed were too much. The potential return did not justify the costs so Roy shelved the project.

Undaunted, their next product development was a promising new type of bottle cap opener that would allow the cap to be resealed. Unfortunately, shortly after the device was perfected, screw-type bottle caps came onto the market, rendering their resealer superfluous.

While Specialty Products was getting nowhere fast, Max Tillman was proving himself to be a valuable asset at Sunbank and was soon promoted to sales manager of the company. Although disappointed that the new products had not worked out as he had hoped, Roy regarded them as simply another learning experience.

"There are a lot of opportunities in the world, but there is also a reasonable opportunity you might fail the first time around," reflects Roy. "And even the second time around, but I maintain that you should not let it stop you.

"Learn from it," he emphasizes. "Don't whine and cry about it. Step back from it and take a hard look at what you did wrong. You may not be happy about the fact that you did it improperly, but your attitude should be that it is going to teach me not to make that mistake again.

"Try, try and try again is the name of the game. If you really want to be successful, don't give up just because you drop through a crack the first time."

Good as his word, Roy was not about to give up on the idea of diversification and expansion. As 1965 came around, he was ready for his first major acquisition; and the lessons learned with his Specialty Products Division would more than repay its costs over the long run.

16
BREAKING NEW GROUND

With the Gross National Products running at over $670 billion, 1965 was the peak of a five-year record run of prosperity in America. Medicare, Voting Rights Act and low rent housing were among ninety bills President Johnson shepherded through Congress.

The world at large paid tribute to Winston Churchill, who died January 24th that year. In Vietnam, the wraps came off. It was the year of the Tet Offensive and by that winter there would be 175,000 U.S. troops in Vietnam with another 40,000 naval personnel in the South China Sea.

That spring, both a Soviet and an American astronaut went for a space walk. Malcolm X was gunned down by Black Muslims for trying to form a breakaway movement. It was the summer of the burning and riot in Watts and the most massive power blackout in history, which left 30 million people in the dark in New York, Connecticut, Rhode Island and Vermont. The following August births were up by 45 percent in those states!

Joe Namath of the New York Jets became the highest paid player in sports history, while Sandy Kofax got another Cy Young Award as he led the way for the Dodgers win over the Minnesota Twins in the World Series.

On a somewhat lesser level than the World Series, Roy Coats continued to pitch softball in the Burbank Industrial League, although with everything else he was doing one wonders where he found the time.

With his new-found confidence and expertise in flying, acquired under the expert tutelage of Joe Wittman, Roy believed the time was right to buy a company plane, rather than continue renting. He settled on a new single-engine Moonie and with it began a grueling schedule of coast-to-coast sales trips.

Mobil display van, Rolls Royce & Moonie Super 21

Organization is the key to successful business flying and Roy made sure that the absolute maximum benefit was squeezed from every trip. A typical sales trip at the time would last two or three weeks. Well before the trip, Roy would line up each appointment in advance, according to his flying schedule.

His first successful round-country trip set the pattern for many others to follow. With his appointment schedule in hand, Roy would take off from Burbank Airport with all the available space crammed with samples and brochures. His first stop was Las Vegas, where he scheduled his sales calls to leave sufficient daylight in hand to fly to Salt Lake City. In Salt Lake City he would check into a motel for the night and begin calls on major accounts in the area the next morning.

The entire trip was set up so that each night he would be in a motel at a set time to put a call in to Sunbank. During the call he would place orders for samples or deliveries to be made and give instructions for the office work needing his attention.

From Salt Lake City his route was to Denver, then Wichita, Kansas City, St. Louis, then north to Chicago, Detroit and Buffalo. From Buffalo he would fly down to Boston, where a large number of major Sunbank customers were located. Here he would visit as many as fifteen or eighteen companies before taking off for the next city.

From Boston he flew down the Eastern Seaboard, stopping at Long Island, Baltimore and then on to Florida. On the homeward leg he called on the shipyards in Mississippi and New Orleans, then flew west with stops in Houston, Dallas and Tucson. Tucson was usually the last stop before returning to Burbank Airport. It was a tiring but extremely effective way to cover an enormous amount of territory. As a result, Sunbank's sales continued to soar. It did, however, throw an increasing strain on his home life.

What made these flying trips so effective — apart from the one-to-one personal contact with the chief executive officer of the company — was the fact that Roy could make instant decisions and not, as many of his competitors had to do, have to refer decisions to the home office. Roy could make these "instant" decisions — which impressed customers — because he had taken the time before leaving California to fully research the likely needs and wants of each customer on his schedule of calls and estimate production and delivery times based on likely orders.

With all this going on, it took a certain degree of guts to once again step outside his own field of expertise, as he had done with Specialty Products. Having proven to himself and others that he could turn his own company around from the effects of bad management (in 1959) and bankruptcy (in 1964) his confidence in being able to do the same for other companies was growing.

When Roy came across a company for sale called Cello Flex, complete with its general manager, Roy sensed another opportunity. He bought the company.

Cello Flex produced air ducts and coupling joints for the aircraft industry. At the time, Rohr Industries had signed a contract calling for Cello Flex to provide $150,000 worth of air ducts for the Gulf Stream II business jets.

Roy chose Max Tillman to work with Cello Flex's general manager and ramrod the Rohr order to completion. Tillman, with no particular experience in this line, was under the gun. The pressure increased when deliveries to Rohr Industries started to fall behind schedule and for no obvious reason Cello Flex started to show a loss in its operations. To make matters worse, the general manager of Cello Flex suddenly announced he had cancer and quit.

Tillman paid a visit to Rohr Industries to renegotiate the contract. Rohr fortunately demonstrated some flexibility in view of the circumstances, but it wasn't enough to prevent Cello Flex from showing a net loss on the contract. To their credit, some fast footwork had enabled them to fulfill the contract under very difficult circumstances and when orders for spare parts finally came from Rohr Industries, Cello Flex did show a profit over the long term. Then a company based in Wichita called Westholt Manufacturing expressed an interest in buying Cello Flex. Westholt was already a customer of Cello Flex and wanted to expand their territory.

Roy and Tillman estimated what it would take them to turn Cello Flex around from its current precarious financial condition into a profitable operation. The figure was too high for Roy's liking. He told Tillman to accept Westholt's offer. Westhold bought Cello Flex and moved the small plant to Kansas.

Initially, Roy had thought Cello Flex would be a good acquisition. On the face of it, from what the previous owners had outlined, it seemed to Roy that stiffer management would turn it around.

"My feeling was, though, that if it didn't work out it was a small enough investment that even if we lost it all, we still weren't out much," Roy explains. "It was intended from the start to be a learning experience. When the opportunity arose to get out of it, I went ahead without a second thought."

Roy forgot Cello Flex and put his attention on a problem he had been mulling over for some time. Because of the many different connector accessories now being produced by Sunbank, a salesman with brochures and a limited sample kit had a very difficult time bringing prospective customers to an understanding of the wide range of possible solutions available to any particular cabling problem. Nor was it feasible for prosective customers to invest the time and money necessary to fly from all over the country just to visit the Sunbank plant in California to gain that understanding.

In many other industries, the solution to these problems is advertising — particularly in trade magazines. For Sunbank, such advertising is not meaningful because it is not possible to condense the multitude of accessories and the complexity of solutions down to the limits of an advertising page — or even a dozen such pages.

Most salesmen would find this an unsurmountable problem but Roy gave it his full attention until he had come up with a workable solution. The solution was to build a mobile sales display van. In effect a large truck fitted with shelves and boards to show the wide range of connector accessories available. The truck could then be taken around the country to customers' plants and an entire engineering and purchasing staff given a quick and thorough understanding of Sunbank's capabilities. In retrospect the idea might seem obvious, but at the time it was far from obvious since no one in the industry had tried it before.

Roy put the idea to some of his top people. Their reaction was mixed. A few said forcibly they thought it would be a waste of time and money.

It should be obvious by now that Roy does not manage his business by committee decisions. After listening to their Pros and Cons, he announced the scheme was sound and would go ahead.

It isn't that Roy doesn't listen to his employees — far from it. He actively seeks their input on problems and decisions. But having trained himself to look over any situation with thoroughness, those with objections to his ideas, or having solutions to offer, had better be able to back them up with equal thoroughness. In this instance, no one had.

Roy knew full well it was a calculated risk, but he believed that if it was carried out well it could have important long-term benefits for Sunbank.

"I've always been willing to push my ideas through," Roy explains, "on the theory that many times the opposition I encounter comes from people who have not put a great deal of thought into the situation in order to understand all the ramifications of what is being proposed.

"Experience has shown me that when you introduce new projects which involve considerable contribution from various departments, that opposition is often based on the fact that the people involved are not willing to put forth the effort required," he adds with a wry smile.

With the introduction of the display truck project, Roy's associates at Sunbank were about to find out that with Roy you are either with him one hundred percent or you'd better

Roy's long time friend — Charles Jones

get out of the way. Roy early on had an intuitive and highly valuable understanding that in a team situation, anyone with counter-intentions to the goals of the team could prove to be more of an obstacle than any opposition from outside.

Knowing there was mixed feelings about the project, Roy took immediate charge and wasted no time. He went out and found a semi-trailer for sale. It had already undergone a partial conversion to demonstrate another company's lighting products. The trailer was fully air-conditioned and self-sufficient, with its own on-board generator. Just what he was looking for.

Even so, it took months of tedious planning — most of it by Roy himself — plus the services of a professional display company to develop the interior. A broad cross-section of products had to be carefully fitted to display boards with space for brochures and additional technical information.

"What sounds like a simple project in the telling was actually a tremendous effort for Sunbank in that we were breaking entirely new ground," Roy explains. Not only did all the products have to fit correctly, but the expense had to be kept within a tight budget — a budget not only for the conversion itself but for the actual road expenses of the truck and personnel manning it who would be on the road for six months at a time.

Finally the display truck was ready to roll. Roy's choice of personnel for the first run was Bert Bergsrud, then sales manager of Sunbank, and Charlie Jones, an employee and personal friend of Roy's, whose capacity for hard work Roy appreciated. Even so, Roy drew up a list of Dos and Don'ts for those involved with the truck and drilled them on the rules as though they were secret agents going out on mission.

* Remember to turn on the air conditioner.
* No drinking whatsoever allowed when running or operating the truck.
* Remember to turn on the circuit breakers.
* Remember to lock all doors when leaving a display area.
* No drinking.
* Make sure the chain is in place around the access ladder.
* Remember, absolutely, positively, no drinking when involved with this truck.

It was a hot spring day in Burbank when the truck finally left on its first tour. All the employees came out to the parking lot to give them a send-off. Roy was so relieved to see it finally on the road he decided to drive into Burbank instead of going back into the office.

"I left the parking lot not more than a few minutes after Bert and Charlie," Roy recalls, "I was driving down San Fernando Road when I saw the display truck parked by the curb. Just then Bert came from a liquor store with two-packs of beer. I was so damn mad I wanted to shoot them both.

"Basically, I had two choices," says Roy, "Either stop my car and fire them both on the spot or just keep going and get my haircut. I decided to carry on and get the haircut. You see, I knew the cab of the truck wasn't air-conditioned and they were about to drive through the desert," Roy adds by way of explanation. "Fortunately, they both took extra care with the truck and we never experienced any problems all the time it was in operation."

The schedule called for three-week tours for each Sunbank salesman. Charlie Jones, however, stayed with the truck as driver for the entire time it was on the road.

In Rochester, New York, Roy joined up with the truck

for his three-week stint. They spent an entire week touring the plants of the Grumman Corporation in Long Island. Before that week was up it was obvious the display truck was an outstanding success. Over the course of the following year, more than six hundred thousand dollars worth of Sunbank products were sold directly as a result of the truck — a figure that snowballed in later years through re-order business.

As a result, thousands of people became aware of Sunbank and its products that would otherwise not have been so exposed. Even twenty years later, brochures and specification sheets given to engineers who viewed the display are still in use for reference and ordering.

The display truck was a concrete example of imaginative thinking. This and other ventures over the years were the product of what Roy refers to as his "dreaming." It is Roy's belief that every company needs a dreamer — but more than that, someone who can not only dream but make the necessary things happen to turn that dream into reality.

Roy works himself hard and by extension expects his employees to work hard also. He is quick to reward dedication and equally quick to show his displeasure toward slackers. One of his managerial assets has been a keen sense of humor, an ability to keep his people at ease while working hard by encouraging good humor in a give-and-take situation; the kind of give-and-take humor that Roy and his Aunt Claudia practiced on each other for many years.

An elaborate and long-remembered example of this befell Andy Allen, then Eastern Sales Manager for Sunbank. Allen, as related earlier, was with Roy on the ill-fated trip to Arkansas to deliver the tractor to Roy's ranch.

As Eastern Sales Manager, Andy did a tremendous amount of driving to customers all over the Eastern U.S. After two years in the same car, Andy was due for another vehicle, and Roy set his plan in action six months before Andy was due to return to California to collect his car and touch base with home office.

Each time Andy called to talk to Roy or someone else at Burbank, he would be given the impression that business was not going well. There would be long sighs and awkward pauses at the other end of the line. The closer it got to Andy's return to California, the more pessimistic everyone sounded.

By the time Andy was ready to drive out to the West Coast, he was thoroughly convinced that business at Sunbank was grim, even though in his own territory sales were going very well. In fact he somewhat tentatively asked Roy if it would be alright if his parents accompanied him on the drive to California. Roy, of course, readily agreed.

The set-piece was an old car belonging to one of the machinists at Sunbank. It had been kept running over the years with bits and pieces salvaged from whatever wreck or junk car happened to be around, totally without regard to matching make or model. A battery had been carried on the back seat at one time and the acid had eaten a large hole in the upholstery.

Where the radio and heater had been there was just a gaping hole. The body was covered with dents and scrapes from twenty years of abuse and one patched fender, covered in red primer, barely clung to the chassis it had been crudely bolted on.

"At the very best," Roy remembers, "that car was an awful mess."

The morning Andy was due to arrive at Sunbank, Roy briefed all the employees on the game plan. He sent the old car to be washed and vacuumed, but nothing else was done to it.

Andy arrived. His sales tour had been excellent, he said, with lots of orders. And, he quickly added, he was certainly looking forward to picking up a new car since the one he was driving had over two hundred thousand miles on the odometer.

"Yes, I know, Andy," said Roy with a poker face, "and it's too bad things are so tough right now that we couldn't get you a really first-class automobile."

"Ah, hell, anything will do," replied Andy. "You know me, I'm not particular. Just whatever you can manage."

Roy picked up the telephone, called for the car to be brought around the front, then took Andy outside. The old wreck wheezed to a halt in front of them.

"Oh, good, you brought the car around," Roy said to the man who got out.

"What the hell is that?" said Andy, with a look of utter disbelief on his face.

"Well, that's what I wanted to talk to you about, Andy," said Roy, putting his hand on Andy's shoulder and keeping an absolutely straight face. "I'm really as disappointed as you are, but things are just so damn tough that when we went out to see what we could afford..."

"And that's it?" Andy asked, incredulously.

"Yes, Andy that's it," Roy replied with just the right touch of feigned embarrassment.

"Goddamn, Roy, that's a little rough," Andy finally managed to say as he walked around the car. He looked at Roy and realized business must indeed be far worse than he thought. "Oh hell, I don't care, Roy. I'll drive anything...but what I drove out here is better than that."

Andy's loyalty touched Roy. He knew all along the loyalty was there, but wasn't sure just how far he could push Andy. As it was, he was having a very hard time not to break down in laughter and give the game away.

"I know it's a little rough, Andy," Roy managed to say, "but we'll make the best of it for now and...after a little while, say a year or so..."

"Yeah," Andy said slowly as the true condition of the car revealed itself to him with each look. "I noticed there's no radio in there, Roy, and those long drives from Baltimore to New York...well, I do enjoy listening to the news and how the weather is going to be...oh, well, that doesn't matter I suppose," he added, not wishing to further discomfort Roy.

"Let's go back inside," Roy suggested.

By the time they were back in the office, the awful implications of what he had seen were finally coming home to Andy.

"You know, Roy, I didn't notice a heater in there either," Andy said.

"Andy," said Roy levelly, "to tell you the truth I don't think there is one."

That was the final straw. "That's it!" Andy exploded, jumping to his feet. "I quit. I'm not driving that goddamn car back there in zero weather without a heater. No sir."

"Andy," said Roy, struggling to maintain a poker face, "You can put on heavy clothes."

"The hell I can," Andy replied. "I'd freeze to death. I'm not going to do it and that's that. I quit!"

"Now you don't really want to do that," said Roy, solicitously. "You know better than that. Come on, let's get some lunch."

The employees had already been briefed by Roy for their performance. One by one, key employees dropped by Roy and Andy's table during lunch to say hello to Andy, and just happened to mention the latest review of sales or production figures. Each would emphasize how bad sales were and generally bemoan the situation with suitably downcast faces.

After an hour of this treatment, Andy finally turned to Roy and said: "Roy, I really feel bad. Everybody here is just working their ass off to keep things going and here I am being a jerk just because of that damned car."

"Well, Andy," said Roy, with great sincerity, "I was hoping you'd see it that way."

When they returned to the office, though, Andy took a second look at the car. Again, the reality was too much for him.

"Roy, I just can't do it, I can't do it," Andy said, storming into Roy's office. "I can't drive that goddamn wreck. What will our customers say when I drive up in that...what if I want to take them to lunch?"

"I don't really know, Andy," said Roy. "I guess we'll just have to figure it out somehow. But right now, why don't you come over to my house and say hello to the children."

Andy was still distraught as they pulled up in front of Roy's house. Andy's attention was suddenly riveted on a brand new Chrysler Imperial parked in front. Roy got out and hardly gave the new car a glance as he walked towards the house. Andy stopped to admire the Imperial. It was loaded with every option — a travelling salesman's dream.

"Wow, that's really something," Andy said to Roy as he walked around the car admiringly. He reached the driver's window and bent down to read the sticker. The car was registered to Sunbank Electronics and the penny finally dropped.

"Why you..." Andy stormed at Roy, as he realized the joke that had been played on him. And then, as the elaborate scope of the six month long joke fully dawned on Andy, both men collapsed in laughter.

"Andy wound up telling that story all up and down the East Coast," Roy relates. "We got a lot of mileage from that little joke. It actually made Sunbank a different kind of company in a lot of people's eyes — a place where the management wasn't just a bunch of stuffed shirts who didn't care much about their employees. It showed we had a kind of camaraderie, and people like to relate to that."

It was this effort of Roy's to make otherwise ordinary events into something special that endeared Roy to his employees, and forged an unusual degree of loyalty.

"Anyone can simply hand over the keys to a new car with a little pep talk and send the man back out," says Roy, "but we would go to great lengths to make something more than routine. I'm not saying it was anything magical on my part. It was just that we were a bunch of young men having a good time at working hard and being successful. This seemed to work out well for us in a business sense as well."

17
COPS, ROBBERS AND VIGILANTES

Roy's idea for the mobile display truck coincided happily with the first successful docking in space and an all-time high space budget of $7.7 billion in 1966. This translated into more business for Sunbank. But it was also a year of unparalleled social upheaval over the Vietnam War and Civil Rights. In California, the gun-toting Black Panther Party was founded and a general air of lawlessness seemed to be abroad in the land.

As 1967 rolled around, Roy and his company were about to become embroiled in some of that lawlessness and violence through a robbery at Sunbank that nearly brought the company to its knees.

Nineteen-sixty-seven was a strange year of many strange years in that decade. Nixon was beginning his drive for the presidency just as the Flower Children came to national attention — Hippies preaching love and a total disavowel of the world around them. Communes and panhandling by young people were the order of the day, as was a growing listlessness and mortality rate among young people from drug abuse. In far away Bolivia, death came to Ernesto (Che) Guevara, Castro's ex-helper and revolutionary prophet — the darling of the street revolutionaries. It was, to say the least, a time of confused loyalties.

In March of 1967 — the same month that Jimmy Hoffa went to Lewisburg Prison for eight years — Sunbank was going flat out. A second shift had been instituted to handle the growing backlog of orders.

Traditionally, the night shift in most companies has been the least productive and the shift most apt to cause trouble, primarily because it tends to be the least supervised by top management. The new six-man night shift at Sunbank was not one of the exceptions.

The first indication that something was seriously wrong was the discovery by Leonard Hauer that the inventory of aluminum bar stock on the racks did not match up with the inventory records. Leonard consulted with Roy and it was decided to place a man on top of the tool crib that night to see what was going on.

The man elected was Jim Lawrence, a machinist who had been with Roy since February 1961. Jim watched as four of the men did the actual stealing of bar stock, taking it out to their cars, while the other two men on the shift just turned a blind eye to what was going on.

The next day Roy fired all six men, letting them know that he considered it a kindness on his part not to turn them over to the police. Further checking by Jim Lawrence indicated that the men were members of the notorious motorcycle gang, the Galloping Gooses.

Wiser from the experience, Roy reverted the operation to an expanded one-shift daytime operation. Two nights later, the thieves returned. This time they broke in and stole every tool and piece of equipment they could move.

The next morning, Roy faced a real crisis. The most critical loss was the specialized tools and gauges needed to manufacture the connector accessories. These were all custom-made for Sunbank and it would be as long as ninety days before replacements could be manufactured — time enough for Sunbank to lose every customer it had.

Roy filed a complaint with the Burbank Police Department, but the police offered little or no hope for the return of the stolen items.

"They told me that within the past forty-eight hours, they had received thirty-five robbery complaints and had neither the time nor the personnel to devote any special attention to our problem," Roy relates.

Roy asked the duty sergeant what would happen if he went after the thieves himself. "If you can find the stolen goods and positively identify them with a serial number or some other mark, call us and we'll take it from there," the sergeant said. He was referring to the stringent Search and Seizure rules under which the police cannot search for evidence of a crime without "probable cause."

That was all the encouragement Roy needed. He went back to the office and called in what would come to be known as the Sunbank Vigilantes: Max Tillman, Charlie Jones, the machinist Jim Lawrence, who also possessed the necessary "street smarts" to narrow down the search area for the thieves. The other member of the team was Ron Hubbard, an engineer who had recently joined Sunbank as a salesman.

Together they began a 24-hour surveillance of the thieves, tailing them all over the San Fernando Valley. When they uncovered what looked like a meeting house for the bikers in an outlying area, Roy would crank up his plane and check it out from the air. Finally it was decided the best course of action was to make a citizen's arrest of one of the gang members in the hope that he would lead them to the others and disclose where the rest of Sunbank's property was hidden.

They caught the thief red-handed with some of Sunbank's tools in his house. The tools had been casually tossed on a mountain of other stolen property that filled his house and overflowed into the yard.

Confronted by five very angry citizens, who were fighting to keep their company and jobs, the thief decided the better part of valor was to tell all he knew.

It soon became obvious that what Roy and his vigilantes had stumbled onto was a major theft ring with operations covering the entire San Fernando Valley. When the thief was booked and the police heard the full story, they became far more interested, even though their hands were still tied by search and seizure rules.

It was arranged that as soon as Roy and his men had positively identified a location where stolen Sunbank property could be found, they would notify the police. The police would wait nearby, but out of sight, while Roy and one of his men entered the house. As soon as they came out again, with positive identification of stolen property, the police could then move in for a full-scale raid and tear the house apart.

What followed was a week out of a cops and robbers television series. By now the thieves knew the game was up and had become very nervous indeed, with the police departments of Burbank, San Fernando and Pacoima on their trail and the five angry vigilantes literally on their tails.

At one point Jim Lawrence was following two of the

thieves in his car when the thieves spotted him and turned to chase Lawrence.

"Well, I stepped on the gas," Lawrence recalls, "did a 180 degree turn, wiped out my muffler on the curb as I jumped over it. I drove out of there like a bat out of hell. I blew two tires and just kept on going. I never slowed for a second and finally they gave up the chase."

Max Tillman, caught in a similar situation, knocked over a fire plug with his car as he made a mad dash with the thieves in hot pursuit.

None of the five, it seemed, gave a second thought to the very real dangers involved in trying to track down hardened criminals, which is probably just as well. It was a textbook "No Guts — No Glory" situation.

In retrospect, Roy realized just how lucky they had been. At one of the houses, Roy and Jim Lawrence decided to kick the door down and take anyone inside by surprise. They kicked down the door and barged in to find themselves in the living room. Standing casually by the fireplace was one of the gang with a rifle in his hands.

Roy describes their reaction as "two minds with but a single thought — get out of there fast!" In far less time than it takes to tell, and with barely a pause in momentum, both men sprinted out of the living room through the kitchen, out the back door into the yard, where a sharp-eyed Lawrence noticed one of Sunbank's tools and grabbed it before vaulting over the fence.

Roy and Jim continued running around the house until they reached the front, then waved the tool at the police hidden nearby. The police moved in quickly, surrounded the house and began a thorough search.

The March 31, 1967, issue of the *Burbank Review* reported:

> "Vigilantes from a local electronics firm closed in on a Pacoima home, rounded up loot they said was taken in a burglary at their company and then contacted police to notify them of the recovery. The action netted return of most of the valuable equipment reportedly stolen from Sunbank Electronics, 2428 North Ontario Street, but police are wondering whether criminal complaints can be obtained

against several of the nine persons arrested at a San Fernando home in connection with the said case. Burbank police officer Bob Wells said the case, one of the strangest in local police history, had been submitted to the District Attorney's office for consideration. He added that serious questions involving search and seizure rules are involved.

Meanwhile police were unable to act in the same manner as the vigilantes because they did not have sufficient 'probable cause.' Police have been prohibited through higher court rulings from acting in such instances. 'These citizens merely acted in good faith. They were familiar with the law and simply wanted their property returned,' Burbank police captain Robert Coveney said."

"The only thing that really ticked me off about the whole episode," says Roy, "was this one guy they caught. He had a loaded gun, was an ex-convict, had stolen goods and marijuana in his possession and for all that the court gave him six months in jail. Hell!"

But revenge or court rulings were beside the point. Because of the courage of Roy and his men, the company was saved from imminent ruin. As a result, morale at Sunbank went sky-high. And, needless to say, the reputation of Roy and his company as being "something special" received another boost which no amount of advertising could have bought them.

18
TRIAL AND ERROR

Popular movies, television and the tabloid newspapers thrive on the dark side of success. The movie stars and headline entertainers, high-flying executives and entreprenurial whiz-kids who have achieved success in capital letters, only to have their personal or home lives fall to pieces around them.

Successful men and women sometimes do have failures in their personal and home lives, but many more strike a balance between the demands of their chosen career and the needs and wants of their family and friends.

Some are fortunate enough, or farsighted enough, to chose mates and friends who remain both understanding and supportive of their ambition. Others try to strike a balance through trial and error... as, frankly, most of us do.

Roy Coats admits his first marriage at nineteen was a youthful mistake. He had no experience or example to follow in how to create a marriage, and so intent was he on making something of himself, of achieving success, that in his own words: "I don't think any woman alive could have put up with me. I was pretty much single-minded about my goals for success..."

At the time of his second marriage, Roy felt reasonably certain that this time he had a wife who understood the demands of his ambition and the necessity to devote a great deal of his time and attention to business. After all, she had worked for his previous employer and knew him on a professional basis before their relationship developed. Of course, there was also the added incentive for Roy that through marriage he could provide the stable home environment he desperately wanted for his two young daughters, following his gaining custody from his first wife, Patricia.

Virginia Coats graduating from William Woods College in Missouri

When his second wife, Joy, gave birth to another daughter, Roy's family had grown to four children — his own three daughters, Ginny; Nancy; and the new baby, Christy; plus Joy's son Scott from her previous marriage.

Unfortunately, Roy's success with his business during those hectic years from 1962 to 1967 was not paralleled at home. The partnership between himself and Joy was going downhill almost in proportion to the rate of Roy's success with Sunbank. If it had not been for the children, it is doubtful the marriage would have survived as long as it did. In retrospect, Roy admits it would have been better for all concerned had they terminated the marriage earlier rather than let it drag on into the bitterness of its final year.

Because of her former background as a secretary with Pacific Automation, Roy had brought his wife into the business as well. When their divorce was imminent, she made an unsuccessful bid to wrest half of the company away from Roy.

Complicating matters still further was the fact that Roy had taken on the care of his ailing Aunt Claudia. After her husband died, Aunt Claudia moved to Seymour, Texas, to stay with Richard Coats (who had discovered the diatomaceous earth). Richard Coats died in 1967. It says a lot about Richard Coats' popularity, that in a town of barely two thousand people, over fifteen hundred showed up for his funeral.

After the funeral service, Roy brought Aunt Claudia back to live with him in California. He couldn't stand the thought of putting her in a nursing home, even though her emphysema had progressed to the point where she required oxygen and her movements were severely limited.

Unfortunately, Roy's wife refused to understand his close attachment to Aunt Claudia or his sense of obligation. She remained cold and aloof, not bothering to talk with Aunt Claudia or even to check periodically on her oxygen supply. This meant Roy had to drive home twice a day to ensure Aunt Claudia was alright. Roy admits that he was heartbroken by his wife's disregard for Aunt Claudia. The marriage was truly at an end.

As it turned out, Aunt Claudia's condition deteriorated quickly to the point where Roy had to place her in a nursing home with round-the-clock nursing care. Right to the end, though, she joked and teased with Roy. When she finally succumbed, it seemed a curtain had rung down on an era of Roy's life.

Following the divorce from Joy, Roy obtained custody of his two older daughters, Ginny and Nancy. It was probably the most frustrating time of his life. Roy admits that it was the only time in his life that he felt utterly helpless as he tried to dress and comb the hair of two little girls and get them off to school each morning. One day he just sat down on the bed and cried with frustration.

Nancy Coats riding Denmark when she was 12 years old. Won several top shows.

Roy knew he needed help. He hired a housekeeper, then another, but it just didn't seem to work. Finally, he called his former wife, Joy, and she agreed to take the two girls to live with her and her own two children. It was not in Roy's nature, though, to admit defeat. In the back of his mind was the conviction that one day he would have his daughters with him again.

Something else Roy had not given up on was the dream of owning his own ranch. He had tasted it briefly in Arkansas, but then had to sell the ranch. Now Ernest Baum brought the idea back in full flower. Ernest told Roy he was selling his ranch in Shadow Hills, not far from Burbank. Ernest was going back to Oklahoma to buy a resort on the shore of Grand Lake, which he was going to call the Iron Horse Resort. Roy didn't hesitate a minute and bought the 40-acre ranch in Shadow Hills, with its rambling house and 14-stall barn and corral.

After Roy moved into the ranch house, a regular visitor was Jim Kaufman, Baum's old friend, who had rebuilt Roy's car without charge when Roy worked for Baum. The talk would always get around to horses, particularly American Saddlebred show horses — Kaufman's passion. Roy started to build up a string of horses and hired a trainer. At one point he had thirty-two, and Jim Kaufman would show up at five in the morning to spend two or three hours with the horses before driving to Van Nuys, where he ran a business with his son-in-law.

Roy's ranch became a popular drop-in spot with his friends, one of whom, Troy Woody, had recently been divorced. Roy offered him the use of a wing of the house. Like Roy, his friends believed in hard work and equally hard play. The ranch became the setting for some memorable parties, but Roy soon got tired of cleaning up after everyone had gone home.

Glancing through the Los Angeles Times one day, Roy was intrigued to find someone with the name Maki Sawaki was looking for a position as house-boy. When Roy called, it was obvious that Maki Sawaki was being extremely cautious. Despite Maki's heavily accented and broken English, Roy could tell that Maki was trying to get reassurance from Roy on a delicate question of sexual preference.

"Well, I'm not queer if that's what you want to know," Roy said bluntly. "And at that point," Roy adds, "I could hear this big sigh of relief at the other end of the line." It turned out that Maki had been propositioned several times already and was getting extremely nervous.

"Maki Sawaki's father was a doctor in Japan," says Roy, "and Maki was the black sheep of the family. He had come to the United States because he wanted to be a writer. He really was quite an asset in such a large house. He took care of the housework and laundry — you'd come home and everything was neat as a pin."

Maki's westernization went into high gear at the ranch. His concept of America as a land of cowboys and limousines was not disabused by coming to work for Roy Coats, for Roy at home looked every inch the American cowboy with his

Tom Worthington in a playful mood

string of horses and free-wheeling friends like Tom Worthington. One day Roy asked Maki if he wanted to go with him to the nearby dump with a load of horse manure. The Tuxford Dump in Sun Valley was home to thousands of seagulls. Each time a truck drove in, thousands of seagulls would take to the air in a screaming flapping crowd, then immediately whirl back down around the truck to await its contents.

"With our horse manure we were very popular with the gulls," says Roy. "Maki had never seen anything like it. He was so intrigued he asked me if he could call all his friends and have them ride out to the dump with me!"

Perhaps somewhere in Japan today there is a book by one Maki Sawaki describing the close ecological relationship between seagulls and American cowboys.

Knowing that Maki was endlessly curious about America, Roy took him on a trip he was making to Oklahoma with Charlie Jones. In Arizona, Maki bought himself a large western hat.

"He wasn't much more than five feet tall," Roy recalls, "and he stretched himself out in the back seat of the car. 'If they could see me now,' Maki said, 'riding in an air-conditioned limousine with this big western hat. My friends they'd say you sonobitch, you sonobitch!' " Roy recalls with a laugh.

One memory of life at the ranch that stands out above many naturally involved Tom (Fuzzy) Worthington. Roy had some business friends from out of town at the ranch for the weekend. They were enjoying a friendly drink when, to his friends surprise, a Cadillac roared up to the ranch with steam pouring out from beneath the hood. The Cadillac, just a year old, slowed to a halt. Out jumped Tom Worthington.

"Roy, call that friend of yours who sells cars in Glendale," Worthington roared. "Tell him I want a new car right now. This damn thing doesn't work anymore."

"The only thing wrong with the car was a broken radiator hose," Roy explains, "but Fuzzy wouldn't listen to reason. Finally I called a man I knew, at Modern Motors in Glendale, by the name of Mister Petapiece. I told him I had a customer for a new Cadillac with all the options and to just drive it out to the ranch and pick up the check.

"So they brought the new Cadillac to the ranch and Fuzzy wrote out a check for the whole amount. All the time he kept mispronouncing the man's name and calling him Peckerpiece. The poor man looked at me, wondering whether to accept such a large check from this wild-eyed, long-haired cowboy or not. 'It's good,' I told him. 'You can verify with the bank.' And that was that. Fuzzy had a new car and my business friends just watched this whole transaction in wide-eyed amazement. They'd never seen the like of Fuzzy in action before."

For a man who loves the wide open spaces, the ranch in Shadow Hills was an ideal set-up for Roy at that time. By western standards, forty acres is a pretty small ranch, but considering that it was only a ten minute drive to his office in Burbank, and only thirty minutes by freeway to downtown Los Angeles, it was a combination that was hard to beat. And even harder to find today. Inevitably, as the 1960s drew to a close, taxes began to escalate at an alarming rate as more and more housing developments pushed out towards the then sparsely settled Shadow Hills and Sun Valley areas. Roy prudently sold parcels of the ranch. By the time Roy came to sell the ranch completely, only three acres remained of the original forty.

Other changes were going on, less noticeable perhaps, but nonetheless real for that. Roy's two previous failures at marriage, and the resulting trauma for his children, left Roy somewhat bitter about marriage and women in general.

"I was awful damn callous toward women," Roy admits, referring to that period following the breakup of his second marriage. "I had a secretary and had to talk to her," Roy adds, "but that was all the women I had to talk to, or wanted to talk to."

In some, such bitterness can last a lifetime, but Roy had always wanted to be part of a family, to have someone who could share the challenges and successes of life. Bit by bit, his self-erected barriers against women cracked and fell away. But not without a struggle.

19
NEW DREAMS, NEW HORIZONS

1968 proved to be the climatic year of that whole angry decade. Martin Luther King Jr., and Robert F. Kennedy were assassinated. President Johnson declined to run for another term because the nation he had promised to mend was tearing itself to pieces. For all his political wiles, Johnson just couldn't put the pieces back together.

There was a senseless orgy of violence in urban centers around the nation. More troops were called out to patrol the streets of American cities that year than the Republic had ever seen in peace time.

Meanwhile, giant transport planes brought home their increasingly heavy loads of coffins from Vietnam. The cost had now risen to 14,592 dead and nearly 93,000 wounded American servicemen. That fall, Richard Nixon squeaked by Hubert Humphrey to become the 37th President.

As the year ended, American astronauts orbited the moon in preparation for the following year's moon landing attempt. In Key Biscayne, Florida, a man called Bebe Rebozo — with too much "Florida for Nixon" campaign money — sank it quietly into improvements at the President's Key Biscayne hideaway, but that would remain hidden from public view until midway through the next decade and an incident known as Watergate.

Perhaps spring that year had something to do with it, but whatever the reason, Roy Coats was about to encounter the woman who would shatter his chauvinistic armor.

Roy was a regular visitor at the apartment of his friend Charlie Jones, in Toluca Lake. Charlie Jones, and another bachelor who had the apartment across the hall, both liked to cook. On Sunday's they were in the habit of preparing large dinners and inviting their friends over to eat and party.

In the apartment above Jones lived Laura Terry, a single girl, then teaching at the San Gabriel High School. Laura was an attractive young woman, born and raised in Michigan amid a large and loving family. At the time, though, Laura was somewhat cool on interpersonal relationships with men.

"I had just not been dating at all," Laura recalls, "because for some reason it just seemed like I didn't fit into the dating scene very well. I didn't like the swinging singles scene at all, so I had pretty much stopped accepting dates."

On this particular Sunday in May, Charlie Jones and his friend were hosting a barbecue party. There were always a number of single girls at these parties and Charlie endeavoured to get any single girls in the apartment building to join in. So far he had no success at all with Laura. That Sunday he decided he would make an extra effort.

A combination of events seemed to conspire to get Laura to the party. She had taken her dog and a new litter of puppies to the beach that morning, carrying the puppies in a laundry basket. At the beach, Laura felt queasy and returned home. To reach her apartment she had to cross the patio and pool area, which meant crossing in front of Charlie Jones' apartment where the party was already underway. Some of the girls at the party spotted the new puppies and rushed outside and again Charlie insisted she join the party.

"When I explained to him I didn't feel well, he called me a stuck-up school teacher," Laura remembers. "He told me I was always ignoring him and that I considered myself too good for everybody else in the apartment building."

Of course, the only way Luara could disprove this charge was by going to the party. She told Charlie she would, but first she had to lie down for awhile. In her own apartment, Laura took some medication and laid down on the bed. A short time later, Charlie came pounding on the door, refusing to take no for an answer. Reluctantly, Laura joined the party, which by now had another arrival — Roy Coats.

Roy recalls their meeting as distinctly casual. "This strange girl came and sat down in the chair next to me and said 'Hi, I'm Laura.' Soon we were talking about this and that," Roy recalls.

Laura remembers trying to ignore Roy and listen to another conversation going on. "Everytime Roy got up to get another drink," Laura recalls, "one of the girls at the party would say: 'Look at that gorgeous hunk of man!' And I kept saying where?"

The party turned out to be a kind of farewell for two girls leaving for San Francisco that day. At some point, it was decided to move the party to Burbank Airport. By now Laura was relaxed enough to accept Roy's offer of a ride.

Laura had forgotten the medication she had taken earlier. On the way to the airport, the combined effects of the medication and the drinks she had consumed began to make itself felt.

"I never get sick and I never throw up," Laura observes wryly. "But that night I threw up all over Roy's brand new Chrysler Imperial."

Roy drove Laura home and kept reassuring her that everything was fine and not to worry about the car, although in truth he wasn't exactly happy about it.

The following day was a hectic one at school for Laura and she came home early and washed her hair. She wrapped herself in an old robe and sat down to grade term papers. Then the bell rang. It was Roy Coats, who had stopped by to see if she was feeling better.

"With all my makeup off as well, I couldn't have looked worse," Laura remembers. "Then my dog bit Roy in the leg. Well, I figured I'd never see him again."

Roy remembers mumbling something about "I'll see you around," as he beat a retreat from the apartment. But despite this inauspicious start, Roy found himself thinking about Laura during the ensuing week. Still not quite understanding why he was interested, Roy telephoned Laura and asked if she would care to go out to dinner. Laura declined with the excuse that she was in the middle of grading final term papers. Maybe some other time, she said.

"I called a couple of days later," says Roy, "and Laura said she couldn't go to dinner because she was just too busy. I said 'I'm getting the message and I'm awful sorry I've been bothering you. I won't bother you again'."

Laura recalls that at that point she felt embarrassed for not simply discouraging his calls at the very beginning. She remembers thinking to herself that on Friday her grades would be turned in and she wouldn't have school on her mind anymore.

"I suggested to Roy we go out to dinner on Friday night,"

Laura explains. "In my head I was thinking that I was going home to Michigan on Saturday to visit my parents anyway, so that will be the end of that."

To the surprise of both of them, they thoroughly enjoyed the evening and each other.

"At the end of the evening I was sorry to see it end," Laura admits. "And after that it was just every time we were together we really had a good time. I didn't go to Michigan until later. I think I was in love with Roy a long time before I even realized it."

One of Roy's characteristics is that generally he does not go about volunteering a great deal of information about his business or personal life. He operates on a strictly need-to-know basis. So it was that Laura had no idea what Roy actually did for a living until their relationship was well developed.

"I didn't know he had two previous marriages. I didn't know he had children," says Laura. "I didn't know whether he had a dime to his name. He talked about flying one night and I asked if he was a pilot. 'Oh, sometimes I fly for a small company,' he said, but he didn't bother to mention it was his plane and his company!"

One night on their way to dinner, Roy had to stop at the Sunbank plant to correct some papers and took Laura inside with him.

"My dad had a machine shop," Laura relates, "so I wasn't terribly impressed with it. I just thought Roy worked there. I didn't think to ask because at the time I still had no intention of becoming really involved."

As 1968 came to an end, they were still seeing each other regularly and liking each other more all the time. Still, it would be another year before they were wed.

"Roy was determined he wasn't going to marry again," Laura remembers. "He was so transparent about it, it was kind of cute. Whenever we were having a particularly good time together, out of the clear blue he would suddenly get very defensive and say: 'Remember, I'm never getting married again.' I'd always pretend I didn't know he was talking to me. I'd look around and say, 'Gee, I didn't hear anybody mention marriage, Roy.' I found out later that a lot of that attitude came from his friend, Charlie Jones," Laura adds with a smile.

By now, of course, Laura knew that in fact Roy did want to remarry, despite his protestations.

"He is a family man, but it was hard for him in a way because he didn't have any role models," Laura explains. "I'm very family oriented. I come from a close family and I believe that was the kind of person he needed — someone who could show him what a family does together.

* * * *

That last year of the Sixties Decade didn't get off to a good start at all. In California, the new year of 1969 came in with record rains and mud slides causing a hundred fatalities in avalanches, drownings or traffic accidents.

That was also the year that hijackers came out of the woodwork to create "Terror in the skies," as the media called it. In May it was shotguns, tear gas and bayonets at the University of California, Berkeley.

It seemed the only thing to cheer about that year was when Neil Armstrong became the first man to step on the moon and plant the American flag. In August, a shocked nation learned about the ghastly Manson murders. Even the Mets went "crazy" that year. After losing one hundred games in the first five seasons, they went all the way to the World Series to win over the Baltimore Orioles. New York, understandably, went wild.

About the middle of that year, Roy finally ended his equivocation and asked Laura to marry him. Laura said yes, but by now there was some justifiable caution on both sides. After talking it over they decided to wait another six months. If they still felt the same way after six months, then the marriage was on.

During one of Laura's visits to Michigan, her parents thought it would be a good idea to travel back with her by train for a vacation; and to meet Roy Coats, of course. Roy met them at the station and Laura's father was not overly impressed. Roy's own car had a flat tire. Typically, Roy borrowed an old rundown car to pick them up at the station and never bothered to explain.

Laura's father was still somewhat cool about Roy until he made his first visit to the Sunbank plant.

"The minute he walked through the door into the plant,

Roy & Laura while visiting England

he lit up like a Christmas tree," Roy recalls. This was all that Laura's father needed to convince himself that Roy was, after all, a "man after my own heart," and they soon became fast friends.

Roy recalls that when he told Laura's father he wanted to marry her, he said: "That's okay, Roy. You don't have to marry her — I'll still come and see you!"

"I told that to Laura," Roy remembers, "and she said 'Well, that's the way his mind works — he really thinks you're marrying me just to get close to him'."

The six months went by and on December 6, 1969, Roy and Laura were married. Together they would finally build the kind of stable, happy home environment Roy had always longed for.

20
OKLAHOMA INTERLUDE

As anyone who lived in or around Los Angeles, or almost any major urban center, during the 1960s can attest, the anger and craziness of that time was enough to make even a confirmed city dweller think longingly about the peace and tranquility of the wide open spaces. For Roy Coats, who had no great love of cities, peaceful or otherwise, his thoughts naturally turned to the country, particularly with a family to think about.

True, the so-called Angry Decade of the Sixties was over, but the new decade of the 1970s hadn't shown a great deal of improvement. The courtroom became a theater of the absurd when the Chicago Seven went on trial in February, 1970. The war widened as American troops went into Cambodia. Then came the demonstrations at Kent State University, Ohio, with four students shot dead.

When Ernest Baum called Roy from Oklahoma and told him he should come out there because there were great investment opportunities, his words fell on very fertile ground.

The explosive growth of the aerospace industry in the 1960s seemed to have settled down and the connector business was now in a steady, more mature growth curve, as was Sunbank Electronics. It wasn't retirement Roy had in mind, but simply to pull back from day-to-day operations and leave that to the managers he had trained.

Another important factor influenced his decision. After his marriage to Laura, they had taken two of Roy's daughters on a camping trip. Laura's strong maternal instincts came into play and in June, 1970, Roy's two daughters came to live with them. Roy believed that in Oklahoma, away from the day-to-day demands of running Sunbank, he could devote more time to his family. And certainly the environment would be more relaxing and infinitely more safe for the two girls than Los Angeles.

Roy talked it over with his wife, then went to visit Ernest Baum. Baum's Iron Horse Resort was near the small town of Grove, Oklahoma, adjacent to the Grand Lake of the Cherokees vacation area. After a tour of the area, Roy decided the opportunities really matched Baum's enthusiasm. Within a short time, Roy bought several hundred acres of land in the area and — to everyone's surprise — a lumber yard.

"People around Grove told me I was crazy to buy that lumber yard," Roy recalls, "but I got to looking at the area around the lake. There were a lot of resorts, private cabins and new home building going on, but no single big lumber yard to service all their needs."

It was another example of Baum's dictum to always keep a sharp eye open for opportunities. Roy also found another resort for sale on the lake and, after discussing it with Laura, Roy bought the resort with the intention of turning it into a home for his family. The move to Oklahoma was on.

Roy turned over the reins at Sunbank to Max Tillman as general manager and Bert Bergsrud, who took over as chief engineer. Roy would, of course, stay in touch with the operation and with the company plane could be in California at very short notice to handle any emergencies.

Meanwhile, the lumber yard was turning into a huge success. Roy scouted for the best prices he could find on wholesale lumber and eventually trucked it in from as far away as Montana. The yard was soon known far and wide for having the lowest priced lumber in the area grade for grade. Even with the low prices, lumber sales showed an excellent profit margin. Within a short time, Roy added another building and a complete inventory of builder supplies.

As an Oklahoma country boy himself, Roy felt more at home in Grove than he ever could in the heavily built-up, industrialized city of Burbank. Roy began to look seriously at the idea of moving the entire Sunbank operation to Oklahoma. Roy may originally have been a country boy, but there was no way he was going to sit back with his feet up or spend the rest of his life fishing.

With the possibility of the Sunbank move in mind, Roy started a small machine shop on the outskirts of Grove. It was to be a trial operation, manufacturing a portion of the

Roy & Laura watching horses at Sunland Stable

Sunbank connector line. It didn't work out. The major problem was labor. In the connector business, dependability was still the key factor and that meant having skilled and reliable workers. The local labor force just wasn't that interested.

"On the first day of the hunting or fishing season, they just wouldn't come to work," Roy explains. "Even threats of dismissal made no difference. The second problem was job training. There had been very little industry in that area of Oklahoma and people with the skills or aptitude for industrial work just did not exist. There was no skilled labor pool to draw from, particularly when it came to qualified machinists."

All wasn't lost though. Through trial operation, Roy gained valuable experience that would be put to good use when the time came in the future to move a greatly expanded Sunbank operation from Burbank to Paso Robles, some two hundred miles north of Los Angeles.

For the time being, Sunbank would have to remain in Burbank. And with that decision made, Roy realized he would have to move back to California. Meanwhile, Max Tillman, Roy's general manager in Burbank and his close personal friend, had visited Roy and Laura and had greatly admired their house and lakefront resort property. The resort business appealed to Tillman and Roy made him an attractive proposition for sale of the house and resort. Tillman jumped at it and today owns a thriving resort business and fourteen-unit motel built to cater to traveling salesmen.

In short order, Roy began to divest himself of his Oklahoma holdings, preparatory to his return to California, while his wife, Laura, and the two girls set about packing and making plans to re-open the ranch house in Shadow Hills. Roy sold the now booming lumber yard to a man he had befriended in the area. The business continued to do very well over the years and is today run by the man's widow. Roy also sold most of the land he had bought, retaining a few plots for his own use.

In was 1972 and Roy was once more firmly in control of Sunbank, wearing the general manager's hat again. The business responded quickly and sales began to climb to new heights.

In the world at large, Vietnam was still grinding on, as were the anti-war demonstrations. In early 1972, Nixon made his historic trip to China, Governor George Wallace of Alabama was shot and paralyzed, and on June 17th that year, five men were caught in a sloppy burglarizing attempt on the Democratic National Committee headquarters in a hotel known as Watergate. It was a name that would come to haunt the Nixon Administration in the coming years, although the incident was overshadowed that November when President Nixon and Spiro Agnew were re-elected with sixty-one percent of the popular vote — a landslide victory.

Back in California, Roy and Laura refurbished the ranch house in Sunland. Then Roy received a call from a business acquaintance who wanted to sell his house in Glendale.

"He told me he needed to come up with some cash, quick," Roy explains, "and that I could make a good deal. Well, I wasn't really that interested because I enjoyed it at the ranch, and Laura and I were doing fine out there."

But the friend kept calling and finally Roy went to see the house. It was more than a house — it was in fact a Southern style mansion that had been used in some of the scenes of the movie, *Gone With The Wind*.

"But I still wasn't that much interested," Roy says, "and he kept coming down on the price, and coming down some

Roy, Laura, Virginia & Nancy in front of Glendale home

more. Finally he got down to what he called his absolute bottom figure. It was just such a good deal I finally bought it."

Roy sold the ranch in Shadow Hills and turned over the redecorating and furnishing of the new house to Laura. They decided the house was so magnificent it deserved loving restoration to its original glory. Over the next year or so, at least one hundred thousand dollars worth of furnishings and an enormous investment of time and effort on the part of both of them went into the house. It was a long, long way from Sulphur Springs, Oklahoma, and the transient trailer courts of his childhood.

During this time, Roy also began to look ahead and formulated some long range plans for diversification and acquisition of new companies. Roy's close confidant in these plans was George Schenk, who had come to work at Sunbank in 1969 as controller. At that time, George Schenk was in his fifties and had a wealth of experience behind him in the day-to-day management of business finance and the all important area of cash-flow control.

Even though George Schenk strongly disagreed with Roy over the Oklahoma machine shop operation, and astutely pointed out the possibility of a skilled labor shortage and the reluctance of many of Roy's key employees to move away from Southern California, Roy had gone ahead with the experiment anyway. For one thing, Roy wanted to try it in the real world and not give up on the idea just because it seemed risky.

"I really respected George's opinions in a lot of ways," says Roy, "but I sometimes think that accountants and engineers are not people who should be in top management because they're too conservative. As a rule, they are unlikely to take a chance on something outside their immediate area of expertise."

With George Schenk as a sounding board, Roy went about looking for a new acquisition. Together they scanned the columns of the *Wall Street Journal* for likely business acquisitions.

As 1973 came to an end, the nation was heartened by the signing of a treaty between the United States and North Vietnam, ending direct American military intervention in Vietnam. American troops were coming home at last.

And something else was coming home to the Nixon Administration and to the nation as a whole. The lid was coming off the Watergate conspiracy as the televised hearings into Watergate held the nation in thrall.

By the end of the year, Nixon's Administration was in ruins, but in the nation as a whole there was a growing feeling of resolve, of the need to clean house and set things in order. Colleges and universities were finally able to resume their role as centers of learning, not revolution. Besides, there was a new and surprising threat on the near horizon. On October 17th the Arab Oil Embargo began and Americans were suddenly brought face to face with the realities of energy dependence as gasoline and oil prices began to skyrocket.

As 1974 came around, Americans found themselves waiting in lines to buy limited supplies of high-priced gasoline. Ahead lay the impeachment and resignation of President Nixon, the swearing in of President Ford and the kidnapping of Patricia Hearst by the SLA — Symbionese Liberation Army.

All in all it was a traumatic if less violent year than many that had gone before. For Roy Coats, 1974 would prove to be equally traumatic personally. Before the year was out, he would come within a hair of losing everything he had worked so hard to build.

21
THE BEST LAID PLANS...

By 1974, Roy had effectively worked himself out of a job at Sunbank. The managers he had were doing their jobs very well, the company was functioning as it should and "I was left with too much time on my hands," Roy recalls.

With the help of Sunbank's controller, George Schenk, Roy intensified his search for a company to acquire and expand. Roy knew full well that his own management theories and practices worked for Sunbank. Now he wanted to test them in another environment.

"There was a desire on my part to see if our management theories were ready for the real world — if they would work with other companies and not just Sunbank," Roy explains.

Together, Roy and George Schenk visited a number of companies for sale, but none of them seemed "quite right." Then Roy came across a company called Air Dry. George was not enthusiastic about it, but Roy felt it had possibilities.

"Looking back on it," Roy admits, "it would be easy to see that George might have been right, strictly on a status-quo basis. Fundamentally, Air Dry was really in a bankrupt position, but I had this feeling we could really turn it around with some of our management ideas. I decided it was worth the risk."

One of the main problems with Air Dry, in Roy's opinion, was that it was being run like a hobby shop. "I think everybody in a buying mood in Los Angeles had looked at Air Dry at one time or another," Roy recalls. "For some reason or other, they had all elected to pass on it. I was just unsophisticated enough to think that perhaps I saw a potential there," he adds wryly.

Roy sat down with George Schenk and other key Sunbank people to review the situation. With business going well at Sunbank, the company had a fair amount of money available for investment that would otherwise be eaten up by taxes. Roy estimated the downside risk at possibly half a million dollars if the company flopped. But if they could turn the company around it was agreed that, with any luck at all, the worth of Air Dry could be boosted to four or perhaps five million dollars.

The asking price for Air Dry would take more cash than Roy was willing to commit though. The alternative was a partnership deal, but Roy's past experience with partners ruled that out immediately. The decision was made to try something different and approach Air Dry with a merger proposition. The offer was quickly accepted.

Air Dry had one major shareholder, who held most of the shares, and a minor shareholder. Each partner received some shares of Sunbank, while Sunbank received stock in Air Dry.

"Based on the owner's representations to me, it looked like a pretty good deal," Roy says.

A series of discussions followed on Air Dry contracts, in particular one large contract with the Ingalls Shipbuilding Division of Litton Industries in Pascagoula, Mississippi. The contract was worth close to nine hundred thousand dollars. It was the largest contract Air Dry had ever received and was equal to their entire total annual dollar volume at that time.

The contract was for the manufacture of a new design of highly sophisticated manifolds. Production would require very close-tolerance machining and testing — a level of expertise that was really beyond Air Dry at that time.

Air Dry's real expertise lay in the production of high pressure dryer systems to keep the air clean and free of moisture around sensitive electronic equipment on board United States Navy ships and submarines.

Roy's main concern was the ability of Air Dry to fulfill that contract, because the company was still involved in minor side projects such as gas conversions for automobiles and deep sea diving compressors, which were draining away valuable time and effort.

Nor was it encouraging to later find out from the previous owner of Air Dry that the Litton contract had been bid on a break-even basis. In other words, the only profit from it would come from later sales of spares and any follow-up orders for new manifolds.

"We ended up finding out that statement was anything but true," Roy explains. "The bid had been made with very little consideration to the real costs."

Roy tightened up the company, unloaded the side projects to eliminate conflicting orders and priorities that had the engineering staff tied up in knots. With these side projects out of the way, Air Dry could concentrate on the difficult development work that was needed on the manifolds; and also concentrate on producing the high-pressure dryers — its real area of expertise and prime source of income.

The next move Roy made was to re-organize the machine shop and bring in sophisticated machine tools and quality control procedures — both vital if the manifolds were to meet the exacting specifications of the contract.

Meanwhile, Air Dry's management had come up with the amount of money they felt was needed to develop the manifolds and get into production — $150,000. Roy came up with the money.

By now, of course, Roy realized that it had been a very poor decision on the part of Air Dry even to bid, alone accept, the contract for the manifolds.

"As we worked our way into the day-to-day operation of the company, it became very obvious that the management at Air Dry had mis-bid the contract so badly it was utterly ridiculous," says Roy.

The hundred and fifty thousand dollars Roy had put into Air Dry was gone in no time. Suddenly Roy was faced with having to come up with another five hundred thousand dollars if they were to have any hope of meeting the terms of the contract.

"I was committed," Roy explains. "There was no way I could back out of it."

To come up with this amount of money, Roy had to get a loan. Not only that, he had to guarantee the loan with his personal holdings, which also included Sunbank and his house.

When the Air Dry merger had first come up, Roy mentioned it to his wife, Laura, explaining that it would be a financial strain for a time and also that there was a risk they could lose everything.

"I said of course, go ahead," Laura recalls. "Roy was the businessman in the family and he's never been one to back away from a risk. He figured the worst that could happen is we would go broke, but we wouldn't die!" she adds.

Unfortunately, the size of the risk did not become fully apparent until after the deal had been signed. Only then were various misrepresentations as to the real state of affairs discovered.

When the need for an additional five hundred thousand dollars arose, Roy went to the two stockholders and asked them to go with him to the bank as co-signers. The minor stockholder, Bob Sheldon, readily agreed. The major stockholder backed off.

"He told me he didn't want to jeopardize his family by taking the risk of losing anything should things go sour," Roy recalls ironically. "My comment to him was that — considering he had misrepresented the whole thing from day one — I wasn't surprised, and obviously he didn't mind jeopardizing my family because I had to guarantee the loan."

In truth, Roy could have had the loan without any co-signers. What Roy was really looking for was whether they were on the team or not.

"When the major stockholder backed down," says Roy with a smile, "we started providing an open door for him."

Within a short time, the major stockholder left the company and a settlement was negotiated to buy back all his stock in Air Dry and Sunbank.

It turned out that Bob Sheldon, the minority stockholder, had been holding Air Dry together for years. Roy now knew Sheldon was on his team and together they could tackle the really hard work that lay ahead to resolve the Litton contract and get Air Dry turned around.

It turned out to be eighteen months of brutally long hours and constant anxiety. Roy began working seven days a week to establish control over the manifold project and keep the rest of Air Dry operating as well. With a total staff of only thirty-five, this meant a hands-on involvement, which Roy preferred anyway. He knew it was the only way to satisfy himself that Air Dry knew what it was doing and would pull out of the crisis. What was particularly unnerving was that there was no way of knowing where the losses would stop. And behind that was the possibility that if Air Dry went into default on the contract, the government — through Litton — could bring claim against Air Dry, which would have finished the company and possibly Sunbank as well.

"What I was trying to do was identify exactly where we stood with the Litton contract," says Roy. "And that was not a minor job. There were literally thousands of components involved and I had to find out the status of each one — where it was ordered from, how much was paid for it, when it was due to be shipped, how many were really needed. Over two hundred different vendors were involved and none of that had been planned or coordinated successfully until we got into Air Dry."

As Roy finally brought order to the confusion, it became obvious that the contract with Litton's shipbuilding division had to be renegotiated. Even so, Roy estimated it would take another six hundred and fifty thousand dollars to complete the contract work. But finally he had a handle on what the bottom line was and could work from there.

A major goof by Air Dry was that they had neglected to specify a series of progress payments — standard procedure with large contracts. Secondly, some of the manifold designs ordered by Litton were so complex it was impossible to build them in those configurations.

Through negotiation, Roy was able to get Litton to agree to make a progress payment of around three hundred thousand dollars. With the true cost of manufacturing the manifolds now in hand, Air Dry shipped between thirty and thirty-five percent of the manifolds called for in the contract.

However, it would still take approximately three hundred and fifty thousand dollars more to complete their obligations, provided Litton renegotiated the contract to exclude the more complex manifolds; and assume some responsibility for the extremely high development cost imposed on Air Dry through the terms of the contract.

"Litton had actually disrupted our manufacturing process over this contract," Roy explains. "They had given us lots of room to make a claim against them."

The disruption from Litton had started before Roy's involvement with Air Dry. The original majority stockholder had sought the advice of a lawyer named Dean Pace on a claim against Litton, but this was later dropped. Roy was introduced to Dean Pace by the major stockholder during a golf game. Roy and Dean hit it off immediately and formed a fast and enduring friendship. Today, Pace is not only a close friend but handles all of Roy's corporate legal affairs.

Dean Pace corporate attorney and good friend

When Roy's letters and phone calls to Litton produced no result, Roy decided it was time to reinstitute the claim to see if that would produce the required reaction and get Litton to take renegotiation of the contract seriously. At that time, Litton itself was having serious problems over contracts to deliver ships to the U.S. Navy, so that the temptation was to ignore a small subcontractor like Air Dry.

Roy asked Dean Pace if he would be interested in handling the Litton contract and Dean said he most certainly was. As an attorney, Dean Pace's specialty is corporate law and he has earned a wide reputation as a highly aggressive, successful lawyer and a tough negotiator.

Finally, Roy and Dean flew down to Pascagoula, Mississippi, for a meeting with Litton executives. Here, Dean discovered that Roy himself was quite a negotiator — in fact one of the best he had come across.

"Most people walk into negotiation without the foggiest idea of their objective," says Pace. "Negotiation is the reconciliation or compromise of known differences. Roy always established his objectives after a thorough analysis of all the data. That's what makes him such a good negotiator."

Despite some heated words in Pascagoula, nothing concrete came of the meeting. Dean finally filed an action against Litton in the United States District Court. It was some five hundred pages long, documenting a claim of some $1.3 million. Realistically, the object of filing so large a claim was to force Litton to negotiate and it worked.

Representatives of Litton from both Pascagoula and the corporate offices in Los Angeles came to the Air Dry plant to negotiate with Roy and Dean.

"Litton pulled a classic negotiation maneuver," recalls Dean Pace, "which is to bypass the negotiator and get the executive who has the ability to settle the matter. They pulled Roy into a side room and offered to settle the claim then and there."

Roy had already determined his objective in the negotiation — it was the amount of three hundred and fifty thousand dollars. This amount was not based on the merits of the claim against Litton, but what he really needed to bring Air Dry out of the red and complete the contract. Litton agreed to pay the amount and the negotiations were over.

Roy's attorney, Dean Pace, was not overjoyed. Pace felt confident that through the courts they could have received many times that amount, but Roy had other priorities.

"Three hundred and fifty thousand dollars would take us free and clear and we could go on from there," Roy explains. "And I think perhaps it was a 'real world' decision to accept that and not push for more through further legal action. Today, Litton Industries Ingalls Shipbuilding Division is still a very good customer of ours. They actually respect us for having the guts to say we're not going to take this kind of crap!"

Roy had what he needed to get the show on the road. And get it on the road he did. He brought in more skilled engineers, better equipment and quality control and got the company to concentrate on dryers and purification equipment. From a company barely managing a turnover of nine hundred thousand dollars in 1974, when Roy took it over, Air Dry today has sales close to twelve million dollars and a staff of one hundred, producing both low and high pressure dryers for military and commercial ships, purification equipment for rocket fuels and the controversial manifold systems.

As a footnote, it is interesting that the major stockholder, who declined to co-sign the loan with Roy, sold out his interest for around two hundred thousand dollars. The minor stockholder, Bob Sheldon, who co-signed with Roy, is today president of Air Dry and his minor stock interest is now worth close to a million dollars. A better example of No Guts — No Glory would be hard to find.

22
THE EMPIRE EXPANDS

By the time of the Bicentennial in 1976, Air Dry was running well and Roy was ready for another acquisition. Richard Nixon had resigned the Presidency the previous summer. The Watergate trial was history and, finally, so was the Vietnam War. It was indeed high time for a renewal of individual resolve and national spirit, both of which had taken a grim beating over the previous fifteen years.

Roy's controller, George Schenk, came across an interesting small company called Delta Flo in San Bernardino. Roy looked it over. The operation was quite small and the price seemed in line, so Roy bought Delta Flo in his own name, rather than using the corporate umbrella of Sunbank.

To celebrate the acquisition, Roy flew the owner to Las Vegas for a weekend of fun and relaxation. Away from business, Roy has an uncanny knack of totally divorcing himself from whatever problems he is handling. If he is playing golf, for instance, then his attention is one hundred percent on the game. And neither has he lost his sense of humor or the ability to playfully tease people, as Laura, his wife can attest.

One time in Vegas, walking towards the Sahara Hotel, Roy challenged Laura to a footrace and gave Laura a head start.

"I just ran like hell," says Laura. "It was hot and all these people where staring at me as I went tearing by. I looked back and Roy hadn't even moved. I was all alone out there. 'You won,' he said. 'It's too hot.' "

On another occasion, Roy challenged Laura to a diving contest. Laura is a good diver and thought Roy was a diver also. Roy got on the diving board first, then simply threw himself in a tumbling, sprawling crash into the water. Laura had no idea what kind of dive it was supposed to be and asked

Roy if it hurt him. Roy said no, it didn't hurt. Then asked Laura if she was able to do the same. "Sure I can do it," she said.

"So I went out and did whatever it was he did. And it did hurt. I swam over to the side and said: "That didn't hurt you?' Roy said, 'Oh yeah, but it's the only dive I can do!' "

Often, on these semi-business relaxation trips to Las Vegas, Roy would take Tom Worthington along, but the former owner of Delta Flo was not the type to appreciate Worthington's brand of humor. Roy wanted this to be a relatively uneventful weekend, so Worthington was not with them.

Even those with a relatively broad mind sometimes found Worthington hard to take. On an earlier trip to Las Vegas with some Sunbank customers, Roy and his guests were in a casino and on their way to the coffee shop. Worthington, three sheets into the wind as usual on these occasions, suddenly keeled straight over onto the floor of the coffee shop as though he had been pole-axed and lay there like a dead man.

Roy paid no attention and escorted his guests to a booth. But management and customers in the coffee shop went frantic trying to get Worthington to respond. Finally, a hotel detective came over and advised Roy that if his friend didn't get up, he would have him arrested.

Roy got up, went over to Worthington and whispered in his ear. As if nothing had happened, Worthington got off the floor, came over to the booth and sat down with a completely deadpan expression. It was, as Roy explains, just Worthington's way of getting a rise out of people.

However, the only so-called "joke" that arose on this particular trip to Las Vegas was after the weekend was over and they were flying back to Burbank in Roy's plane. The former owner confessed he had misdirected Roy somewhat. Before the contract was signed, Roy had specifically asked the owner if there were any problems with safety or government standards concerning the duct heaters. The owner had assured him there were not.

Now the owner confessed that there was indeed a problem with the safety and quality of the units. For a brief moment, Roy was tempted to open the passenger door and tell the man he could walk home.

"I didn't care much for the fact the man had lied to me,"

recalls Roy with admirable restraint. "But I felt with the engineering expertise available to me at Sunbank we could overcome any problem involved."

Roy asked his top tool and die maker, Leonard Hauer, to take a look at the duct heaters. Leonard actually laughed when he saw the amateurish way the units were put together. Within a week, Leonard had designed a totally new heater assembly that was not only more durable and reliable than the original unit, but could be manufactured in a third of the time through use of the jigs and patterns he had drawn up. Within a short time after this, Delta Flo was operating at a substantially improved turnover and profit level.

Roy's growing empire now included his original company, Sunbank Electronics' North Hollywood Screw Products — a multi-spindle automatic shop that had been a subcontractor for Sunbank for some years before Roy bought the company in 1976; since then the company has steadily expanded with a very healthy profit performance. There was also Royal Die Casting, which had originated within Sunbank and was later spun off as a separate company. It primarily services Sunbank's needs, but also sells its services to outside companies.

Meanwhile, Sunbank Electronics had again outgrown its facilities in Burbank and was operating in two locations — the Corporate Headquarters building on Empire Avenue and the Sunbank Electronics production plant, in a new building on Winona Avenue in Burbank. Then, with overseas business on the increase, Roy formed Sunbank International Products to become the overseas marketing arm for the entire Sunbank Family line of products.

All of these companies were doing well enough by now that Roy could again turn his attention to the idea of a dream ranch. Jim Kaufman, his old friend from the days of working with Ernest Baum, went on scouting trips with Roy. Kaufman had earlier interested Roy's wife, Laura, in show horses. She proved an exceptionally adept student and within a short time was bringing home first place ribbons with regularity.

In the beautiful rolling hills of San Luis Obispo County, some 200 miles north of Los Angeles, Roy found what he was looking for — 1800 acres, with a small ranch house and all the out-buildings for cattle and horses. Roy bought it and

Roy telling about the rock picker at Rainbow Ranch

named it the Rainbow Ranch, after seeing eight double rainbows flickering over its rolling hills one day after a rainstorm.

Although well into his seventies by then, Jim Kaufman agreed to be Roy's ranch manager. Horses and cattle were bought and installed and Roy and Laura set about refurbishing the ranch house and buildings. At long last, Roy could get back to the kind of work he really considered a pleasure — constructing a workshop and horse stalls, wrestling with a bulldozer or, best of all, climbing up on top of a mechanized rock picker to clear the fields for crops.

It wasn't too long before they decided that the ranch was where they wanted to live permanently.

"It looked like a beautiful place for Laura and me to live and to build a home for the children," Roy explains. "It is also close enough to Los Angeles that I can easily travel back and forth to the plants in Burbank and San Bernardino. The drive takes approximately three and a half hours, but to fly between the Paso Robles Airport and Burbank only takes fifty-five minutes, so it is really pretty convenient. And the country, the lifestyle, is something that means a great deal to me personally," Roy adds.

All told, it took three years for the dream to come true — eighteen months planning the new house and working the design so that all the furnishings they had invested in the home in Glendale could be incorporated into the new house. It was then another eighteen months hard work before the new ranch house was ready for occupancy.

The rambling 6,500 square foot ranch house was the final realization of Roy's boyhood dream. Sited atop an imposing ridge, the stone and cedar house commands an eagle's view of the rolling ranch lands. The stone that figures prominently throughout the house is "Sonora driftwood" — a rugged-looking dark brown sedimentary rock from the Sonora desert in Northern Mexico. Roy and Bill Terry Jr. drove the truck and semi-trailer to Sonora for the tons of rock needed. The driveway is a replica of some of the streets Roy and his wife saw on a trip to Portugal — tens of thousands of square-cut colored stones set in mortar. Roy cut and set the first few thousand stones himself to give the masons a clear-cut pattern to follow.

As if he didn't have enough to do, another company was brought to his attention by a friend. The name was Hughey and Phillips. It was a small company manufacturing airport landing and hazard lights. Although small, the business

Roy with 2 puppies at Rainbow Ranch

1½ years to design, 1½ years to build — Rainbow Ranch house was the realization of a lifelong dream, for Roy

seemed to be on a sound footing and the owner ready to retire.

This time, Roy determined that one of his managers at Sunbank should get some experience at taking over a company and bringing it into line with standard administration and modern management techniques.

Roy chose Ron Hubbard, an engineer who had joined Sunbank in 1967 as a salesman and then progressed to sales manager. Roy put Hubbard in charge and told him to handle the situation. The only stipulation Roy made was that the company had to show a twenty percent annual growth with fifteen percent profit. It did and Ron Hubbard is still in charge of Hughey and Phillips.

As the new ranch house came close to completion, Roy put the Glendale house up for sale and bought a condominium in Burbank to use whenever they needed to be in town overnight.

In 1981 Roy, Laura, and his two daughters moved permanently to Paso Robles. The house was all they had imagined it would be and more.

"I get up in the morning and I can see twenty or thirty deer walking across my fields from the kitchen window," says

Roy, with obvious delight. "It is really beautiful country."

It was so beautiful and the style of living so well suited to Roy's temperament, that a new thought occurred to him: why not move the Corporate Headquarters of Sunbank to Paso Robles? Roy realized that with the new computer system being installed, everything could be easily monitored from Paso Robles. With capable people in charge at each company, the whole Sunbank Family of Companies, as it is now known, should continue to operate as before.

Roy didn't know it at the time, but that decision set in motion a chain of events that would soon have him working harder than he had ever worked before. It was a move, however, that would not only strengthen Sunbank over the long term but could, in the future, prove to be a crucial advantage over his competition.

23
ALWAYS A STEP AHEAD...

"When you start out with nothing, you have to try harder," says Roy Coats. It is many years since Roy Coats has had to try harder because of economic necessity or the sting of personal survival — as was the case during his early years — but that attitude still prevails. And it is a very healthy attitude to have if one is engaged in business.

For one thing, conditions change and what worked last year does not necessarily work this year. As an entrepreneur par excellence, Roy Coats knows that taking risks goes hand in hand with opportunity. The successful entrepreneur, however, is the one who does everything he can to minimize those risks and goes all out to capitalize on the opportunities.

The daring and complex procedure of moving the entire Sunbank operation two hundred miles north, from its original location in Burbank to the small rural town of Paso Robles, better illustrates why Roy Coats has been so successful than almost any previous example.

Before getting into that move, though, another example of Roy's ability to change — in this case his own lifestyle — is pertinent.

It should be obvious by now that Roy Coats likes to play as hard as he works. While Roy has never condoned drunkenness per se, for most of his life he has thoroughly enjoyed drinking with his friends. In that respect, he is the "epitome of a man's man" as one of his closest friends describes Roy.

Roy has always separated his business and pleasure so that one does not interfere with the other. Nevertheless, a "little traveling music" as Roy calls the apricot brandy he used to drink, was part of the high pressure, cross-country lifestyle he lived for so many years while building up Sunbank's sales organization, along with the cocktails at lunch and the celebration sessions at the club bar following a hard game of golf.

It used to be that when Roy was hiring a new salesman for the company, he had his own unique way of testing the applicants. After the preliminaries were over and before the final decision was made, Roy would take the prospective salesman down to a local bar and talk it over in a more relaxed atmosphere.

"We would play some pool or whatever, and I would keep buying the drinks. I did it just to see if the man could keep his composure even while pretty drunk," Roy explains. "If he could keep himself together drunk, then I could feel pretty confident that he wouldn't embarrass himself or the company once he was on the road on his own. If he couldn't hold it, I wouldn't take him on."

Regardless of how one feels about such a test, the truth of the matter is that a few drinks with a client is part and parcel of a salesman's life.

"I learned from my own years in sales," says Roy, "that clients always want to go for a couple of drinks. It's part of the routine and if you have a couple yourself and get to a point where you might say some things you shouldn't, or do something silly, then that is no good. It gets in the way. I always felt a good salesman could hold himself together in any social situation," he adds.

"The truth is I drank too much and until the time I met Laura I was pretty damn wild," Roy admits candidly. "As a matter of fact, a lot of my friends have commented over the years that until I met Laura I was sometimes a little difficult to be around. The last fight I got involved in was within a week or two of meeting Laura — and hopefully the last fight I will have in my lifetime. I was in my early thirties then and hopefully a little smarter in regard to life...and beginning to realize you don't want to run around punching people or being punched because of disagreements. It could also have something to do with the fact that the very last fight I had I was kicked in the face — the first and only scar on my face in all those years. I realized then I had not exactly been too smart in the way I dealt with people in the past."

But although Roy had changed his ways as far as being all too willing to settle disagreements with his fists, he still continued drinking and here the law of averages caught up with him.

In 1978 Roy was stopped by the California Highway Patrol and issued a citation for drunk driving. A skillful defense by attorney and friend Dean Pace avoided the more serious consequences of such a charge, but Roy still had to attend a traffic school.

"I wasn't looking forward to it," Roy admits, "but they showed a film of professional drivers and how just one or two drinks affected their driving. These drivers, who I had to admit were a hell of a lot better drivers than I am, were knocking over pylons and weaving around like crazy after one or two drinks. And the thing was, they were really trying to do it right. I realized then what a hell of a chance I'd been taking all those times with the 'traveling music' and just made a completely cold, rational decision to quit drinking altogether.

"The only regret I had was that I was just starting to develop a taste for really fine wines," Roy admits. "But I have to say that my marriage and my business have both benefited quite a bit as a result of giving up alcohol."

It was about this time also that the idea of moving not just the corporate offices but the entire Sunbank Electronics business to Paso Robles began to form in Roy's mind. Roy knew from his previous experiment in Oklahoma that the key to any such move was the availability of skilled or trainable personnel.

The idea of conducting a survey came to Roy after getting thirty or forty replies to an advertisement for a new ranch manager — many of them with a background of skills that was surprising in such a rural community. The new foreman was to replace Jim Kaufman who had finally decided to retire at the age of 79.

Roy surveyed the Paso Robles-Atascadero-San Luis Obispo area and as far up the California coast as Monterey. What he found was a surprising number of very trainable people living in the area.

An advertisement for an engine lathe operator, for instance, drew as many as twenty replies. In Los Angeles, Roy found he was lucky to get one or two because of the intense competition for really good workers.

Behind this idea, of course, lay a more cogent motive than

simply the convenience of having Sunbank in the same area where Roy now lived. After twenty-three very successful years in business, Roy as usual was looking ahead.

"I knew the business was going to be more competitive in the future," Roy explains. "There is really no company that doesn't go through changes in their corporate history. Sunbank, after twenty-three years, has gone through a revamping of the whole connector accessories marketplace.

"In the early Sixties we were in a market whereby if you produced quickly — if you were there first with the most — you could get a good dollar for it," Roy adds. "Over the years, the government agencies that control the kinds of things we sell have been trying to bring about standardization, to document certain testing requirements on our products. And what it really has started to do is to create a market whereby you've got to be very thoughtful of the market changes taking place."

To meet this change, Roy believed his companies must be equipped with the finest machinery available, so that production could be maintained at a high rate under really effective cost control systems.

"I feel I can attain those things better in Paso Robles than I can in Los Angeles," says Roy.

One of the reasons for this relates to the quality and willingness to work of the available labor force — a quality which Roy believes has deteriorated substantially in Los Angeles over the years he has been in business.

"I also found there were a lot of good people who would like to move up there — get out of the city with their families and away from all the problems connected with big city living," Roy elaborates. "And so, looking at the future of this business, knowing it is going to be far more competitive, I just want to be in a better position than my competition five years from now.

"I feel strongly that there is a good possibility that, in five years time, only the fittest are going to survive," he adds. "And I want to be among the fittest."

Change, of course, tends to be upsetting for some people, for not all welcome change as enthusiastically as Roy Coats. It was natural enough, but still disappointing to Roy, that when he first began the initial restructuring of Sunbank in 1980, preparatory to the move, some of his key employees didn't exactly see things the same way.

What had occurred, apparently, is by no means unusual in successful companies. The early days of fish-and-fumble were over and Sunbank had settled into a steady growth pattern. If complacency is going to strike, this is the time it shows. Roy had delegated more and more responsibility to his top managers as he got involved in new acquisitions and in the construction of his new ranch. Then, in 1980, he got the feeling that perhaps some of them had become complacent. The dynamism that always infused Roy's companies seemed to be missing.

"I wasn't satisfied with the results," Roy explains. "But when I would try to discuss it with some of my top people they would get just out and out indignant. And I'm just stubborn enough to say, 'Hey, you know, if you're not part of the solution, you're part of the problem.' " Another of Roy's operating rules. What these managers had failed to understand was that Roy felt a responsibility to all his employees, and not to just his managers, to see that the Sunbank Family of Companies continued to be a viable growing business. So Roy went about handling the problem in his own unique fashion. He rolled up his sleeves and began to lay his big capable hands on the day-to-day operations of Sunbank. What Roy did, in effect, was to plunge right in and start to work around the managers who were digging in their heels. They had the option of changing tack and enthusiastically assisting Roy to restructure the company or continuing to be indignant and self-righteous.

"Of course, right away I got next to their egos," Roy explains, "just by virtue of going in and starting to work around them. And their egos said, "Hey, I won't put up with this crap,' and within a short time three of the problem managers resigned.

"Some of them felt I couldn't do it anymore," says Roy, as he reflects on the opposition he got to his restructuring and revitalizing of Sunbank. "But they forgot one little thing — I started the company originally and had structured and developed the company they were managing."

With three top managers gone, Roy had to take up the slack at Sunbank, in addition to riding herd on the move of the company from Burbank to Paso Robles.

Meanwhile the results of the surveys were so positive, Roy decided to open up a small plant to test whether the labor situation was in truth as good as it appeared to be from the survey.

For some years, Roy had been using sophisticated Numerical Control (NC) metalworking machines in the Sunbank and Air Dry operation. He decided to move about a dozen NC machines to Paso Robles to test the feasibility of establishing a separate Numerical Control division to support Sunbank and Air Dry.

Roy hired a manager and started out with eight employees on a single day shift. This worked so well that over a period of only three months the small plant graduated to three eight-hour shifts, five days a week.

The fact that he could operate a night shift productively was very encouraging. As Roy had discovered to his cost in 1967, when the newly-instituted night shift at Sunbank robbed the company of all its tools, maintaining a night shift in Los Angeles or any other big urban center is extremely difficult to control. Even the larger companies who can afford to maintain expensive supervision, report that production on night shifts drops markedly in comparision with normal day shifts.

The stage was now set for the big move, but to pull it off required a tremendous amount of intricate planning. As Roy explains, "My function in all of this was to make sure that we had it all planned right down to the gnat's eye and to verify that the managers who were controlling it at both ends had all the communications necessary in order for this not to fall flat on its face."

Roy realized that what he would have to do is move the operation to Paso Robles in bits and pieces, and to do it very swiftly. At that time, Sunbank was working with about a five million dollar backlog of orders. They could not afford to miss even one day's production; any disruption had to be kept to the absolute minimum.

For half a year, units at the Sunbank plant in Burbank were moved to Paso Robles. The machinery would be in operation one day, dismantled and loaded onto the semi-trailer that evening, driven the two hundred miles to Paso Robles, re-installed that night and be ready to go back into production the next morning. At the same time, new personnel had to undergo intensive training and be ready as the machinery arrived.

The first such move consisted of the final assembly operation. Next came the entire stock room with all the purchased parts inventory, which amounted to hundreds of thousands of components. This meant computer terminals had to be installed in Paso Robles and tied into the main Burbank computer because the inventory was computerized. During all this transition, personnel were being shifted from Burbank to Paso Robles, new people hired in Paso Robles and sent to Burbank for training.

"We'd bring them to Burbank for two or three months," Roy explains, "train them and get them back to the plant in Paso Robles just about the time the truck was due to arrive there with the equipment they were to work with."

By the end of summer, 1981, the Numerical Controlled machine shop was in operation, as was the new plating facility and the final assembly operation, producing a limited amount of production. The final part of the move was made the following year, transferring all production equipment, computers, engineering and customer services to Paso Robles.

Just how grossly Roy's managers had under-estimated his capacity to dive right back in and handle the day-to-day operations can be judged from the fact that, after the stock room and computers had been moved to Paso Robles, Roy went into the plant every morning at 6:30 a.m. to work as an expediter, frequently not leaving the plant until 8 or 9 p.m. at night.

"I wanted to satisfy myself that we had restructured our computer program in such a way that it was actually functional," Roy explains. "My wife, Laura, even came in to operate one of the computer terminals and she really loved it. I have never seen a substitute for hands-on understanding of what the hell is going on in your plant," he adds. "And during the time of the big transition, it was just a matter of everybody there had to do their share. That's pretty much the way we function. It doesn't matter at Sunbank what your title is, if it is necessary to get a job finished then you might find the general manager helping someone do a rather menial task."

When pressed, Roy admits that from 1980 until the final move of all Sunbank production and shipping was completed in 1982, "I worked harder than I ever did before — even when I was starting out in business."

Momentous though this decision to move to Paso Robles was, Roy approached it in exactly the same way he approaches all his business decisions — by relating percentages to the successful outcome.

"I say that if I'm successful in my major decisions about eighty percent of the time (perhaps a little less than that) more than likely I'm going to be successful," Roy explains. "I say to myself, okay, what are all the factors that affect this decision? What is the worse condition we could run into? Then, without going into blue sky dreaming, what could be the best condition? And then I use everything I have available to me that affects that particular decision — I call in all the best brains in the company and we talk about it. I pull out any ideas that are available. We list them down and take all the positives, all the negatives, and anything else that comes up. Then everybody goes away and I sit there and say to myself — well, you haven't screwed up too badly yet, so now we've got to figure out what the screw-up factor is in this deal."

During the move to Paso Robles, Roy came across a prime example of what he calls the "screw-up factor." Two years earlier, they had ordered a new type of automatic machine that cost fifty-five thousand dollars. The decision to buy it was based on the manufacturer's claim that this new automatic machine would build 450 parts an hour, eight hours a day without having to fuss with it.

Delivery was supposed to take place in eighteen months. Six months after the delivery date had passed, it finally arrived at Sunbank.

"We couldn't even get it to work, much less build 450 parts an hour," Roy says. "So the company sent all their experts out, who said they didn't really understand what was wrong, but they had screwed up somewhere. They loaded the damn thing on a truck and shipped it back to New York.

"Six months later they called us back and said they finally had it running. I said that was super, since it had been two years since we bought it. Then they told me there was one minor problem — we were only going to be able to get 350 pieces an hour. Not only that, we would have to change the tap every two hours because there was going to be a great deal of wear. And at the end of the shift we would have to resharpen all our tools."

Roy said he would get back to them. He discussed it with his engineering staff. When everything was taken into account the conclusion was they would be lucky to get 160 parts an hour, plus an operator would have to check and adjust the unit constantly.

Roy went back to the files to check on alternatives. The alternative considered at the time of ordering the new machine was to buy a used automatic machine and partially fabricate the parts at the rate of 350 an hour, then transfer to an automatic tapping machine which could do the final tapping at the rate of 850 an hour.

"So we cancelled the order," says Roy. "I told them to keep it and we bought another used automatic for twenty-nine thousand dollars, instead of fifty-five thousand for their unit. We took a twenty-five hundred dollar bath on the deal because we had given them a fifteen hundred dollar deposit two years earlier and then paid about a thousand dollars for shipping. But I felt we were better off to give up the twenty-five hundred and not be saddled with a white elephant.

"This is the kind of decision-making we have to do in our company that is relative to our success. We could have been messing with that machine for five years trying to make it produce. Instead, we elected to take an alternative route real quick and have something that is desirable."

Today, the Paso Robles operation is working at full capacity, fabricating and shipping all Sunbank products for both domestic and overseas customers.

"The only thing about the whole move that got me down," Roy admits, "was that I lost my controller and good friend, George Schenk. George developed bone cancer in 1980. In January of 1982 he had a heart attack and although he fought it like hell, his body was just too beaten down by the cancer, and he died. He was a fine man, an excellent controller, and a very dear friend."

With the move to Paso Robles complete, Roy had also accomplished the reorganization and revitalization of the company. He created a new management team with a vice-president to handle all the Sunbank Family of Companies in Southern California, and a new president responsible for the Sunbank Plant in Paso Robles.

"I can again pull back from the day-to-day operations," says Roy, which gives him the time to work on building up his registered herd at the ranch, taking time out for trips to Europe with his wife and buying a second condominium unit for vacations in Hawaii.

But when Roy Coats says he has pulled back it can be misleading. He still commutes regularly between Paso Robles and Burbank in the spanking new twin-engine turbo-prop plane; he can still be found in the Sunbank Family new corporate building in Burbank several days a week.

It should also come as no surprise by now that Roy has also managed to find time to start yet another enterprise — Sunbank Development, Inc. — in Paso Robles. To have a construction company of his own has been a dream of Roy's ever since he swabbed hot tar on roofs as a helper on his discharge from the Marine Corps.

The secret of Roy Coats is that he likes to create. For Roy Coats there are few things more satisfying than watching a house or building grow and being able to see the physical results of one's efforts.

After being in operation only six months, Sunbank Development has...but that's another story.

24
THE DREAM GOES ON...

It should be obvious by now that while this story does have a beginning, it does not have an end in the sense that Roy Coats is already off and running with a totally different kind of business venture, having formed his own construction company.

Fictional characters are often far easier to define than their "real life" counterparts. For one thing, the novelist can create "facts" to suit the situation, can create his characters from a wide combination of traits or, alternatively, concentrate on one major trait to the exclusion of all others.

Defining Roy Coats is not an easy task, even for his closest friends, one of whom describes Roy as "an enigma." This enigmatic picture of Roy was particularly evident during the years of his boisterous social life which appeared to many to be in such contrast to Roy Coats the "solid businessman."

Yet at no time is there any evidence that Roy's "wild side" ever interferred with Roy the businessman. Roy's wife, Laura, has of course observed Roy in business and social settings, under extreme stress and in the flush of success.

"Roy has many good traits," Laura says, "but if I could pick one of his traits for my own it would be his single-mindedness, his ability to concentrate. I know of no one else who can concentrate like Roy...zero in on what he is doing so that everything else ceases to exist. We can be playing tennis and he'll come off the court with a blister that's bleeding. And you would never know it. He's out there playing and he really doesn't feel it."

The ability to divorce himself from events peripheral to the task at hand is a learned trait — the product of application and discipline.

Roy listening to good friend Sam Soghomonian

Laura recalls an excellent demonstration of Roy's attitude. On a trip to Europe Laura mentioned to Roy she wanted to call home to make sure everything was alright.

"Laura, what are you going to do if you find out the roof is leaking...worry about it all through Europe?" Roy asked.

Laura didn't call home and in Europe was amused to find American businessmen "running all over themselves to find a telephone to call home or to find a New York newspaper. Roy never looked at a newspaper, not once," says Laura. "He said he just didn't want to know and if there was an emergency we would hear about it anyway."

Perhaps the most objective view of Roy Coats comes from Sam Soghomonian a teacher with more than 30 years experience, the last 18 years at Pasadena College where he is a full professor. His background is political science. Sam and Roy became good friends when two of Roy's daughters attended Mayfield, a private school in Pasadena. Sam's daughters also went to Mayfield and both Roy and Sam served as members of the Mayfield Board of Trustees.

"Roy fits into the classic mold of self-made Americans," according to Sam. "He put it all together with perseverance and stamina and incredible perception. Roy found out early in life 'there is no free lunch in America' and discovered the formula early in life — that you can do it, can climb any mountain you want if you just take it one step at a time. And he did it. As a result, Roy is an idealogue. He is opposed to deficit financing. To Roy it has overtones of freeloading and he is opposed to that. What makes this country exciting is the blending of the dreamer and pragmatist, the dreamer and the worker, with our objectives always farther than our reach will go."

Sam views Roy Coats as one of the most generous people he has ever known. And yet, he points out, many people who know Roy socially have no idea just how wealthy Roy is because he doesn't flaunt it in any way.

"One time I ran out of wood," Sam recalls. "We had two fireplaces and barbecued all the time...I think it's an

Nancy Coats into the beer at party at Glendale home

Christy Coats works at a Sunbank family company at age 21

American idiosyncrasy," Sam adds. "One day Roy found out I didn't have any firewood. He called a friend of his, got out his own truck and chainsaw and spent an entire rainy day with me and another wealthy business friend cutting down one of his trees for me. He could have bought 13 cords of wood for me with the money in his pocket. I mean, what an enormous act of generosity, because his time is more precious than his money."

Over the next decade or two it would not be at all surprising if Roy Coats just keeps on expanding into new ventures and new successes, for if there is any "secret" to Roy's success, beyond his No Guts — No Glory philosophy, it is this: Roy Coats loves to create. How he creates has been the story of this book.

Roy Coats has been a success because he has always been willing to dream, to dare, to take risks, and to persist. And, most important, willing to learn from his own experiences and that of others — in other words a willingness to change.

An individual who has lost his faith in creating, in bringing his dreams to realization, will generally be found to be holding on to what he has, no matter how little that is. He begins to hold what he has closer and closer to himself. He resists change, will not reach out to embrace new ideas and challenges; from that attitude alone an entire catalogue of failures could easily be devised.

Change is the only constant in the physical universe — from the sub-atomic through to the level of a galaxy. While history is but a shadowy mirror of that change, nevertheless its lessons would seem to be obvious: an individual, a business or even a nation that resists change, will not adapt to it, will eventually be plowed under.

The history of man's civilizations is a catalogue of attempts to resist change and the results can be seen in the ruins of Greece, Rome, Alexandria and a thousand others. A more recent and perhaps more pertinent example is that of the American automobile industry, which stubbornly resisted the change to smaller, higher quality and more fuel-efficient cars. An industry that once dominated automobile manufacturing world-wide almost went completely under in less than a decade. Only now is it struggling back to a sound economic footing, but at the cost of losing most of its overseas and a good part of its domestic markets to foreign manufacturers — to say nothing of the grief it brought to American workers and investors.

Roy Coats has a keen understanding of change and the need to predict those changes and modify his plans accordingly. To change is to survive.

It is also true that Roy Coats had perhaps a lot more incentive than most of us to study the problems of change. From an early age he knew clearly that he wanted to change his life from one of abject poverty to the level of a decent life, at the very least.

At fourteen, he decided he wanted to be a success, to make "something" of his life. At twenty-three he achieved that success, but even then realized how fragile success can be without a solid base. But, obviously the acquisition of a fat savings account was not the extent of Roy's ambition.

He wanted success in terms of achievement — the kind of fulfillment that comes when one knows one has stretched one's talents to the utmost and brought into being by sheer

Roy claims he got a par on this hole

strength of will and persistence that which one set out to accomplish, regardless of obstacles.

An important part of that achievement for Roy Coats is that in doing so he has created opportunities for others to prosper as well. Over the years he has been more than generous with his advice and help. Indeed, the main motive behind this book is to encourage others to reach out and dare to turn their dreams into reality.

As Roy said during the research for this book, "If just one person reads this and says to himself: 'If Roy Coats can do it with all he had going against him, then I can do it too,' then this book will have been worthwhile."

March, 1984